CW00695604

THE CHRISTIAN CITIZEN

THE CHRISTIAN CITIZEN

by

H. F. R. CATHERWOOD

HODDER AND STOUGHTON

To
Dr. D. Martyn Lloyd-Jones

INTRODUCTION

THIS BOOK CONSISTS of a series of talks, all except one of which were given at the annual graduate conference of the Inter Varsity Christian Fellowship of Canada at Lake Couchiching, Ontario in August 1967. The one exception, Chapter 3, 'The Salt of the Earth', was a talk given at the triennial conference of the International Fellowship of Evangelical Students at Wuppertal, Germany, in the same month.

I have kept the style of the talks in the book, because to do otherwise would have meant more revision than I had time for in a fairly busy life. The talks were meant to provoke discussion and so they are somewhat more dogmatic and unqualified in style than they would have been had one set out to support all the argument in a proper academic way. They are also, of necessity, more racy and more personalised. These talks do not set out to prove their argument up to the hilt. They try rather to sketch out a part of Christian doctrine which seems recently to have been neglected by rather a large part of the Christian Church.

Those to whom I talked were almost all Christians and graduates, so the talks assume a certain knowledge of the Christian faith and an assent to its truths, together with a position of potential leadership in the Church and in society.

However, I hope the book will be of interest to all who are concerned with the basis of ethics in society and its relation to law, to government and to the quality of life and of personal relationships.

While there are wide differences of view today amongst those who profess the Christian faith, there are even deeper differences between Christian and humanist and in developing the argument one cannot but be conscious of the different bases on which different people will ground their assumptions. It is possible to deal with this either by taking one's own, honestly held, position; or by trying to aim at the lowest common denominator of agreement. The latter is the more popular line in the Oecumenical mood of today, but I have chosen the former because, though there are large areas of agreement, there are areas of disagreement too wide and too deep to be glossed over. Indeed it is only as one begins to spell out the application of Christian principles in society that one realises what a gulf has opened between the Christian ideals and way of life, and the life and practice of the world today.

I am most grateful to Wilbur Sutherland and to his executive committee for all the help they have given in the production of this book, to Hywel Evans, to my wife and Oliver Barclay for reading the manuscript and for their very valuable suggestions, and to Ruth Sowton for transcribing the tapes into type.

Balsham, Cambs.   Easter, 1968

CONTENTS

CONTENTS

CHAPTER I

The Need for Christian Involvement

THE MAIN THEME of this book is that the Christian should be actively concerned with and involved in the world outside the Church. The great changes created by industrial society have put into the melting pot the patterns of life to which our religious institutions have for so long been adapted and this makes the theme especially urgent.

Now of course many professing Christians are heavily involved in the affairs of the world. Many outside the Church may think such a book unnecessary. To the politician, the world seems full of 'turbulent priests' and he wishes that they would tear off their clerical collars, their symbols of higher Authority, and come out and meet him in a straight fight. We see clergymen, bishops and moderators making passionate political speeches — while politicians exhort us to do good with a religious and moral fervour. But the outsider does not hear the many Christians who react against this and feel that the Church of Christ is not of this world and should keep out of its quarrels and arguments. They do not see why Christians should take time away from the work of telling the gospel to others, from the cultivation of a good and holy life, from family worship and instruction, to become involved in economic and political issues which, for the most part, they feel to be worldly in the worst sense and therefore right outside their interest. Just as there was a reaction from the worldliness of the Catholic Church in the Middle Ages, when men founded monastic orders to get away from it all, so today the Church faces a similar Protestant pietism, which regards the world as wicked, a place in which the righteous have no part and where the only work which will not eventually perish is the salvation of the souls of men for eternal life. This book is not meant to encourage the tub-thumping television cleric whose proper job is the cure of souls, but to encourage more Christian laymen, who are entitled to take their place in public affairs, to come out of their protective isolation and do their public duty.

It is no part of this message to minimise the Christian's care for the salvation of men's souls. That is as important as ever. The duty of care for our neighbour is undivided. If we care for his body we will also find that we care for his soul. If we really care for his soul, we should find that we also care for his body. The best Christian missions have enormous social influence. It is not true Christianity but false pietism which divides one from the other. The social life of the pietist tends to be centred exclusively on his family and Church connection. He may live in the same town as other folk, ride in the same trains, walk the same streets, work in the same laboratory, but beyond the needs of earning his livelihood his circle and their circle hardly touch at any point. In the anonymity of today's great cities you do not have to live in a monastery to be monastic; just as the monk would think it wrong to vote or to be involved in public issues, so our modern pietist will almost certainly not be found signing his name to a petition on a controversial issue of the day. He may possibly vote in the secrecy of the ballot box, but many would regard politics as a dirty game and would not bother to vote at all. He will, of course, be charitable and may give generously but his money will go almost exclusively to churches and missions. It will more often go to save men's souls for eternity than to help their bodies face the hunger and the pain of time. He is aware that there are problems in the world. He reads his newspapers and he cannot help but see them round about him. But his answer is the answer of the cloister. It is the answer of prayer and not of action. He asks that God should do something, or should move somebody else to do something, but for him it is enough that he should pray.

One would think that if he was not concerned for men's bodies, his concern for their souls would force him at some point to engage with the world as it is. But the man of the world does not much care to have those preach to him who are not also his genuine friends and, on the other side, the pietist, self-isolated from social contact, finds that it is now possible by modern means of communication to reach vast numbers of people with a message without actually knowing any of them personally. So his evangelism ceases to be based on real love and friendship of man to man and woman to woman, but is based on time hired out on commercial radio and television and on vast evangelistic campaigns. In campaign audiences of ten thousand or twenty thousand a night extended by closed-circuit television to thousands more, the man preaching the message and the person hearing it never have the remotest chance of a personal encounter and the enquirer is left face to face with a stranger to answer his questions about the greatest and most personal event a human being confronts in his whole life. Not all big campaigns have this flavour and there are genuine converts even in those which do, but the pietist relies on them too much to do his work for him.

Maybe I exaggerate to make the case; maybe there is no Church or community where Christians are so utterly disengaged from what goes on around them. But these temptations are present to all Christians and we do not always resist them. Nor is it just that we succumb to the temptations of pietism. There are underlying currents which drive us this way.

One of the most important of these currents is the disengagement of business life from social life. In the old days, and in a small community, a man's business life and social life went together. The same people were involved and he could not help it. But today a man can earn a living without ever meeting anyone he knows in his home or Church. Indeed he can earn a living without most people even knowing where or how he earns it. There is a Sherlock Holmes story of a blind beggar who is locked up by the police. At the same time a well-heeled commuter disappears from a London suburb, last seen getting off the train in the City of London. Holmes discovers that the beggar in the police cell, who refuses to wash, is the commuter in his workaday disguise. But what was a barely conceivable tale in the world's largest city at the turn of the century is a good deal more credible in the megalopolis of industrial society seventy years later.

A second driving current is social segregation. In modern

cities this is becoming much firmer and is damaging the relation between Churches and society. Churches which move out to one-class suburbs become Churches not of young and old, rich and poor, newcomer and old inhabitant, but become instead a one-class Church. There always was a right and wrong side of the railroad tracks, a west end and an east end; but the one was never very far from the other and all could go to the same Church. But no modern developer would put a fifty thousand pound house or a twenty thousand pound house in among the five thousand pound houses, nor would anyone in most cities today build an expensive house in a slum area. When the immigrants move in, everyone else moves out – and everyone so often includes the bulk of Church members.

But I feel that Christians would not have gone along with these patterns of society had there not also been a wrong trend in some key doctrines. So there is a third trend at work. In the last hundred years a small part of the Church – but especially that part which has held to the principle orthodox doctrines of the Reformation – has been very heavily influenced by some extreme dispensational theories. There are a wide variety of these theories and I do not pretend to know them all – especially those of the more cataclysmic kind. Most of them however have seen the world as given over increasingly to evil, matters getting worse and worse, Armageddon close at hand and the Day of Judgment not far behind. The world was beyond repair, 'evil men and seducers waxing worse and worse' and to try to do anything about it would be to fly in the face of an inexorable trend in human affairs. Instead of the prayer 'Thy will be done on earth as it is in heaven', there set in a pessimistic and ennervating pessimism.

A fourth trend has been the reaction of orthodox Protestants against the involvement in worldly affairs of the liberals at the one extreme – whose social gospel seemed to be not much more than a thinly disguised humanism – and at the other extreme the Catholics who in Europe have gone so far as to found their own political parties. The orthodox Protestant might well feel that if Catholics and liberals were in error on other things they were probably in error in this too. But many who accept the full

Christian gospel have failed, I think, to balance the doctrines of separation, prayer and evangelism with the very clear statement by Our Lord that we are to love our neighbours as ourselves. This Commandment is not only just as binding as the other doctrines, but is ranked by Our Lord second only to the Commandment which tells us to love God with all our heart. Our Lord was at once asked 'Who is my neighbour?' and the answer showed that he was not our fellow-churchman but someone left suffering and impoverished at the side of the road. The story went on to show that it was not the churchmen, the orthodox believers, who helped him, but a stranger outside the circle of the Church. Just as the Pharisees, though they wanted to be an exclusive social group and to ignore the problem on the other side of the road, were a part of Jewish society, so the Christian Church today is part of the society in which it lives. And just as the Pharisees were judged by Our Lord on the way in which they fulfilled their responsibilities to that society, so the Church is judged by its performance and practice towards our society today.

I suppose that two of the most orthodox Protestant Churches today are the Southern Baptist Church in the United States and the Dutch Reformed Church in South Africa. Yet the world does not judge them on their orthodoxy but on their reaction to one of the great social problems of today, which is racial prejudice. I do not in the least want to condemn those Churches or to minimise their problems. It is the essence of the Pharisee and hypocrite to condemn sins to which he is not exposed or tempted and condemnation of racial discrimination by countries not much troubled by racial division, smacks somehow of hypocrisy. I do not even say that the attitude of these Churches to this great social problem is the best test of their Christianity. All I want to make is the limited point that they are in the very middle of the issue and that they cannot avoid it by concentrating on prayer or personal piety. Many of these big issues spring up unannounced and if the Church has not been aware of the social problems around it, it is taken off-guard and unprepared. Individuals may be able to react quickly, but whole Churches do not change their attitudes overnight. Instruction takes time to give, opinion takes time to form and meanwhile it becomes only too evident to all onlookers that a Church which is supposed to teach eternal truth is painfully becoming reconciled to truths which had been apparent for some time to many who were not Christians. If Christians did not form political opinions, or if they kept quiet about those they did form in private, no great damage might be done. Too often however they pick up the nearest prejudice which happens to be lying around, and although they consider it wrong to undergo the discipline of taking a public position, they are more than happy to air these views in private and the cumulation of their private views cannot be hidden. A senior member of a leading Church in a North American city greeted a stranger and foreigner in the Church with the view that American politicians were making more and more concessions to the negro. The more the negro got the more he would want, but politicians could not think of anything better than competitive bids for his favour. The stranger said that he thought the 1964 Republican candidate, Barry Goldwater, could hardly be said to have been very strong in the bidding. This caused a momentary pause, followed by the clinching argument, 'But then he didn't get elected.' The stranger carried away from that Christian Church a strong taste of racial prejudice.

A Church which does not attend to contemporary problems tends to become identified in its outlook and presuppositions with the established orthodoxy of ideas for the time being. And in a society where the political leadership embodies the orthodoxy of ideas, the Church becomes identified with the political leadership too. There is a real danger that Christians may unthinkingly conform to the pattern of power and wealth in society. Then when the established orthodoxy of ideas is questioned or the leadership is overthrown the Church suffers damage as well. When the Communists took over in Russia in 1917 they identified the Russian Orthodox Church as a power of the Tsarist establishment and the Church suffered with the Tsarists. It may be that the Catholic Church faces today the same dangers in South America. The Catholic Church in Italy and Germany has come under violent attack since the last war for its attitude to the Nazis and Fascists, though, in passing, it is only fair to say that the very structure of the Catholic Church and the need for uniformity in every country puts it in a better position than most Protestant Churches on the issue of race relations.

Not only can a Church subconsciously follow the orthodoxy of ideas, it can get caught up in a fleeting contemporary mood. When Britain went to war in 1914 many people, in the militarist mood in which Europe was caught up, regarded the pulpit of the Established Church of England as being one of the most effective recruiting grounds for the new volunteer army. When that army was massacred on the Somme in 1916 and in the third battle of Ypres in 1917 there was a violent reaction and revulsion against war and with it an equally violent reaction against the Church which had sent men to war. To be involved in the affairs of the world means that our critical faculties should be more and not less sensitive. We need to stand back from the dominating pattern of our own society, the industrial society in which we live, and to decide whether or not we really agree with that pattern. If it does not fit with Christian principles then it will be better for us and for the Christian faith if we say so sooner rather than later.

On a more personal level it is hard for the outsider to distinguish today's doctrine of rigid separation from the world from an attitude of indifference to the world and its problems. The Christian is here to be the 'salt of the earth'. He is to be 'a light to lighten the world' and no one is going to be of any influence or enlightenment if he seems already to have removed himself from this world to the next. I do not believe that we can get round this problem by mass-production evangelism. Evangelism is and should be intensely personal and the work of winning others to the Christian faith is inseparable from the personal care and the endless patience which one genuine friend will show to another. This is not something which can be packaged and sold through the mass media.

What this generation seems to lack above all is a partnership between the clergy and the rest of the Church membership in the work of evangelism. I remember a friend of mine newly

2

appointed as a curate in the Church of England who said after a few weeks in his first parish that he could see what, in the divine order, he was called to do but, for the life of him he could not see what function or purpose God had given to the rest of his congregation. The answer is, I am sure, that if the Church is to engage with society then the individual members of the congregation are the cogs which engage. Without them the man in the pulpit will whirl away with little effective result. The job of the ordinary Church member is to bring the world and his wife to Church and through the Church to God. He can do this by love and friendship; but he can also do it because he seems to have a better concept of society, a better sense of justice and purpose in the world in which they both live.

Western society is living today on the accumulated moral capital of Christianity. Throughout the centuries Christians have been in the forefront as men of ideas, as men who have shaped society as they thought the Christian faith demanded. They may not always have been right; indeed, they did not always agree. None the less a Christian consensus emerged and the society we now have in Britain, Canada, the United States and other similar countries is largely a result of their efforts. The respect for the dignity of the individual, religious toleration, the emancipation of women, the rule of law, the scientific method, universal education, the habit of work and the habit of thrift, all these owe a tremendous debt to past generations of Christians. But if the Christians of today fall out of the battle of ideas, the world will not go on just as before. In place of Christianity we already have humanism, empty, pessimistic and finally, I believe, forced by its lack of religious sanction to become authoritarian or perish. We have Communism, feudalism, racialism, existentialism and mysticism. This interim period has been dubbed the secular society, but a secular society cannot by its nature last for long. Men were made to believe and if they do not believe truth then they will believe error. Our Lord has told us that if you cast out the devil and leave the house empty then seven devils worse than the first will come in and occupy the empty space. Men want an ideology and what they want they will have. I do not think that the milk and water of humanism can ever hold man's imagination and will. Other full-blooded ideologies are likely to be too strong for it. If the Christian influence were to continue to grow weaker, then on current trends we are far more likely to have a passionate racialism—that is why it is vital that Christianity shall not be identified with the white races, but can be seen to be a faith where 'there is neither Jew nor Greek, there is neither bond nor free'.

The Christian should have no fear of stepping into the world of affairs. Men of faith have been there before him. Joseph was a ruler in Egypt. Daniel was a ruler both in Babylon and Persia. Moses was one of the greatest law-givers the world has ever known. David was a soldier and Solomon one of the world's greatest sages. But the greatest example is the Founder of our faith, the Lord Himself. He clearly cared for the people around and they rallied to Him because He cared. He healed the sick and befriended the poor. Although the Apostles as spiritual leaders did not pronounce on secular politics, the Epistle of James is full of blistering social criticism. I believe, therefore, that the case is made for a re-emphasis in our generation on the Christian's responsibilities as a citizen.

CHAPTER 2

God's World or the Devil's?

ANY EXAMINATION OF the Christian's position in the secular world must start with the question of God's relationship to the world which He has created. Despite its fallen state the world is still God's creation and despite man's fall into sin the stewardship of God's creation is still man's divinely appointed task.

This stewardship was God's first command to Adam and Eve. In Genesis 1: 27–30 we read 'So God created man in His own image, in the image of God created He him; male and female created He them. And God blessed them, and God said unto them, Be fruitful, and multiply, and replenish the earth, and subdue it: and have dominion over the fish of the sea, and over the fowl of the air, and over every living thing that moveth upon the earth. And God said, Behold, I have given you every herb bearing seed, which is upon the face of all the earth, and every tree, in the which is the fruit of a tree yielding seed; to you it shall be for meat. And to every beast of the earth, and to every fowl of the air, and to every thing that creepeth upon the earth, wherein there is life, I have given every green herb for meat: and it was so.' Then came the fall of Adam and afterwards the great catastrophe of the flood, but God made a new start with Noah. Despite the fall of mankind the commission to Noah was almost the same as that given to Adam before Adam's fall. Genesis 9: 1–3 read 'And God blessed Noah and his sons, and said unto them, Be fruitful, and multiply, and replenish the earth. And the fear of you and the dread of you shall be upon every beast of the earth, and upon every fowl of the air, upon all that moveth upon the earth, and upon all the fishes of the sea; into your hand are they delivered. Every moving thing that liveth shall be meat for you; even as the green herb have I given you all things.' So God's purpose for man's life on earth before the fall still stands undisturbed for the generations after the fall – and since it was given it has never been cancelled.

Not only are we told to administer God's creation but since God has made us in His own image, He has given us some part of His creative ability. It is this spark of creativity and this authority over nature which marks man out and which enables him to carry out his commission. There is nothing so deeply satisfying in human life as creative achievement, nothing which so makes us feel that we are fulfilling our basic function in life. All the New Testament teaching on work confirms this basic command to men. Paul says in II Thessalonians 3: 10–12 'For even when we were with you, this we commanded you, that if any would not work, neither should he eat. For we hear that there are some which walk among you disorderly, working not at all, but are busybodies. Now them that are such we command and exhort by our Lord Jesus Christ, that with quietness they work, and eat their own bread.' In the first Epistle (4:11–12) he writes 'And that ye study to be quiet, and to do your own business, and to work with your own hands, as we commanded you; that ye may walk honestly toward them that are without, and that ye may have lack of nothing.'

While this world lasts God both upholds the present creation despite man's sin and deliberately withholds the full natural consequences of sin. God undertook to Noah and his descendants that there would be no great catastrophic flood like the one which wiped out the antediluvian civilisation. He sends the rain upon the just and upon the unjust alike. So much, indeed, do the ungodly prosper that the faith of the Godly can be shaken. A whole Psalm is devoted to this theme. In Psalm 73: 3–5 we read 'For I was envious at the foolish, when I saw the prosperity of the wicked. For there are no bands in their death: but their strength is firm. They are not in trouble as other men; neither are they plagued like other men.' In verse 13 he says 'Verily I have cleansed my heart in vain, and washed my hands in innocency.' But then he begins to understand and in verse 17 we read 'Until I went into the sanctuary of God, then understood I their end.' And in verse 20, 'As a dream when one awaketh; so, O Lord, when thou awakest, thou shalt despise their image.' One of the great attributes of God is His long-suffering. It is in the nature of men to want to see quick results but it is in the nature of God to give man every chance to repent.

If God has not written off the world, who are we to do so? And if God cares for mankind in its sinful state, who are we to withdraw from the wicked world? There remains much of the original glory in God's creation. As the Psalmist says 'The heavens declare the glory of God; and the firmament sheweth His handywork.' But the brightest constellation of all should be the Christian Church. This is God's true glory and it is through the Church that God wants to show His love for mankind and His longing that they should be reconciled to Him. It is therefore not only no part of the Church's duty to duck out of the world but it is a very central part of its function, part of its very being, that it should in real and practical ways show God's love and care for the world around.

But the Church is not God's only means of sustaining creation in the face of sin and the fall. God has given us effective instruments to sustain His creation in spite of the destructiveness of sin. The most basic of these instruments is the family. There would not be time to go through the Bible to illustrate the importance of the family. It is everywhere. It is in the Ten Commandments, it is in the detailed law given to the Children of Israel, it is in the teaching of Our Lord and it is in great detail in the letters of the Apostles to the Churches. The duties of husband to wife and wife to husband; parents to children and children to parents. There are the rules of consanguinity in marriage aimed at protecting the wider family from emotional upset and division. To its great credit the Catholic Church has seen the importance of the family and does everything in its power to protect it. Whatever its errors, this is not one of them. The protection of the family as the basic unit of society is one of the great issues of our day and one in which Christians should be heavily involved. This is perhaps one of the deepest issues which divide the Christian from the humanist. For though the humanist also wants to protect the good in family life, his attitude to divorce, to homosexuality, to abortion, and to pre-marital intercourse are all different from the attitudes of the Christian and produce in practice very different results. The link between delinquency and the lack of a family background is plain for all who want to see. I need hardly spell out the many forces in our lives today which are hostile to the ideals of family life. They are too numerous and too evident to be worth a catalogue.

The second great instrument of God for order in a disorderly world is the institution of government. The ancient Jews were given secular laws which they had to obey on pain of penalty from the magistrate. But government is still a divine institution, even where it is not linked, as the Jewish government was, to the Church. In Romans 13: 1–7 Paul tells us 'Let every soul be subject unto the higher powers. For there is no power but of God; the powers that be are ordained of God. Whosoever therefore resisteth the power, resisteth the ordinance of God: and they that resist shall receive to themselves damnation. For rulers are not a terror to good works, but to the evil. Wilt thou then not be afraid of the power? do that which is good, and thou shalt have praise of the same: For he is the minister of God to thee for good. But if thou do that which is evil, be afraid; for he beareth not the sword in vain: for he is the minister of God, a revenger to execute wrath upon him that doeth evil. Wherefore ye must needs be subject, not only for wrath, but also for conscience sake. For this cause pay ye tribute also: for they are God's ministers, attending con-tinually upon this very thing. Render therefore to all their dues: tribute to whom tribute is due; custom to whom custom; fear to whom fear; honour to whom honour.'

Paul was not talking about a constitutional democracy with one man and one vote. He was talking about a great and arbitrary Imperial power, the Roman Empire presided over by an autocratic and heathen Emperor. He was telling the early Christians that whatever their feelings might be as sub-ject and conquered people, they owed the Emperor the duty of obeying his laws and paying his taxes because it was God who ordained his office. Now of course this doctrine raises problems. The Emperor was not God and when he claimed to be God he had quite clearly exceeded the authority which God had given him. Although the Christians owed him a duty to obey his laws they did not owe him a duty to worship him as God. This they refused to do and they were right. At this point they could say with Peter 'We ought to obey God rather than men.' So the doctrine of the divine right of earthly rulers requires at least one qualification. But this and other qualifications—of which today almost all of us are aware—must not obscure the essential doctrine that earthly government is of God and requires the respect due to a divine institution.

Thirdly, God has put something of His divine law into men's hearts so that however hardened they may be there is a realisation that right is right and wrong is wrong. Paul tells us in Romans 1: 19–20 'Because that which may be known of God is manifest in them; for God hath shewed it unto them. For the invisible things of Him from the creation of the world are clearly seen, being understood by the things that are made, even His eternal power and Godhead; so that they are without excuse.' And in chapter 2: 1 'Therefore thou art inexcusable, O man, whosoever thou art that judgest: for wherein thou judgest another, thou condemnest thyself; for thou that judgest doest the same thing.' And in verse 14 'For when the Gentiles, which have not the law, do by nature the things contained in the law, these, having not the law, are a law unto themselves: which shew the work of the law written in their hearts, their conscience also bearing witness, and their thoughts the mean while accusing or else excusing one another.' I remember once listening to an argument between two Members of Parliament, one a Catholic and the other a humanist. The humanist wanted to back a Bill for the abolition of legal penalties for homosexuality. The Catholic pressed him hard to find out whether this arose from his own moral concepts or from the wishes of the great body of people living in his constituency. It was fairly clear that the argument that the instincts of the ordinary man and woman in the constituency would be against the Bill whatever the intellectual arguments put forward by the humanist. There is more of the law of God written in men's hearts than we will sometimes admit.

Finally, God has ordained the Church as an earthly institution in which His people meet together and which is to be the 'salt of the earth' and the 'light of the world'. All Christians know and understand that the Church's job as the light of the world is to proclaim the truth to all who will listen. What I do not think we understand so fully is that the Church must also function as the salt of the earth. It is the Church's responsibility to prevent the corruption of the body of mankind which tends to take place where evil is not countered by the law of God. So pervasive has been the influence of Christianity in the world that there must be few places where the teaching of the Church and the influence of its members have not had some effect. It is where some violently anti-Christian ideology has temporarily gained power that the evil underneath is suddenly and horribly uncovered and one realises the reality of the restraint which was exercised by Christian influence. And though much evil has been done in the name of Christianity, everything in the teaching of Our Lord and His Apostles contrasts with the wrongs of mankind, under whatever name these wrongs are perpetrated.

I believe that the premillennial theory in its most extreme dispensational form has been one of the influences responsible for the withdrawal of many Christians from the world and its affairs which I regard as being contrary both to the teaching of the Bible and to the older traditions of the Church. Nor is its hopeless and catastrophic view of the world borne out by the growth in influence of Christianity over twenty centuries. Indeed the Church may, as the centuries pass, have even more impact on the world. Christians are taught by Our Lord to pray 'Thy will be done on earth as it is in heaven.' We should believe that God can and will answer this prayer, so we should not give up in the face of worldly opposition, but should press on in the belief that the God who made the faith so powerful can make it more powerful still.

To sum up, I think that we must believe as Christians that 'The earth is the Lord's and the fulness thereof.' That it is the

Christian and not the man of the world who is the true cus-
todian of God's world. He is the man of affairs, the key to the
safety and prosperity of mankind. The Christian exercises his
custody by the influence of his actions and by what he says,
helped by the power of the Spirit of God in him and in the
consciences of men. He does not do it by arrogating government
to himself alone but by operating within the framework of the
society which God has laid down. Evil continues present in the
world but it can be restrained by the greater influence of good.
What we find around us is a very long way from heaven; but
it is also a very long way from hell.

We do not want to do injustice to the case for Christian
withdrawal from the world. We must in fairness quote the
verses which they would quote. Our Lord says of His disciples
in John 17: 16 'They are not of the world, even as I am not of
the world.' James tells us in chapter 4: 4 'The friendship of the
world is enmity with God.' John tells us in his Epistle, chapter
2: 15–17, 'Love not the world, neither the things that are in the
world. If any man love the world, the love of the Father is not
in him. For all that is in the world, the lust of the flesh, and the
lust of the eyes, and the pride of life, is not of the Father, but is
of the world. And the world passeth away, and the lust thereof:
but he that doeth the will of God abideth for ever.' However,
these passages do not really contradict what we have been
saying. From the passage in John in particular it is clear that
the world here is not the physical world and the people in it,
but the state of mind of men and women who care for nothing
and live for nothing but the society in which they find themselves. The Christian must balance the earthly and the divine.
Worldliness as described here is an unbalanced attitude which
can only see the earthly and which ignores the divine. 'The
world' in this sense means the earthly, godless outlook. In John
17: 15 Our Lord says 'I pray not that Thou shouldest take them
out of the world, but that Thou shouldest keep them from the
evil.' In I Corinthians 5: 9–11, Paul writes 'I wrote unto you
in an epistle not to company with fornicators: yet not alto-
gether with the fornicators of this world, or with the covetous,
or extortioners, or with idolaters; for then must ye needs go out

of the world. But now I have written unto you not to keep company, if any man that is called a brother be a fornicator.' It must be clear from both these passages that although there is evil in the world this is no excuse for the Christian to stay out of the world. The Christian's earthly acts are balanced and instructed by his knowledge of divine law. These laws are meant not only to keep him from worldliness but to make sure that what he does in the world is good and effective.

The object of the Christian must be balance. The temptation is always to go to one extreme or the other. The pietist may be at one extreme, but at the other extreme is the worldly Christian. Each extreme confirms the opposite extreme in its prejudices. If anyone is to blame for the extreme withdrawal of the pietist, for the hothouse Christian who will not venture out to meet the world, it is the worldly Christian. He may set out with the best intentions, but he is soon swallowed up, undistinguishable and useless. We may not always agree with the methods and poke bonnets of the Salvation Army, but when they went into a pub or a bar, there was never any doubt about their position or motive. They were in the world, but they were not of it. They cared for the sinner, but not for the sin. A uniform may be provocative, but it can also be a protection. People respect the Salvationist or the nun and will not expect them to dishonour their position. For the ordinary Christian, anxious to be friendly but not to go along with the crowd, the position is not so easy. Yet those who are friendly but stick to their principles will be respected for their courage and will have an influence quite disproportionate to their place in the human scale of values.

CHAPTER 3

'The Salt of the Earth'

I SHOULD LIKE, now, to take up from the last chapter the Church's calling as one of the divine institutions for the preservation of human society. The two outside tasks of the Church, the preaching of the gospel to society and the work of preserving society as it is found on earth, go together and must not be separated. Our Lord not only taught, He also healed the sick and fed the hungry. This was an essential part of His ministry. It was His way of showing people that He cared for them. His message was not just 'pie in the sky'; when they were hungry, He wanted them to have bread and fishes here on earth too. It was His disciples and not Our Lord who suggested that the multitude should be sent away empty. So a Church which appears to care for men's souls without caring for their bodies cannot claim to be following the principles laid down by its Founder. The great English social reformer of the nineteenth century, Lord Shaftesbury, once said 'When people say that we should think more of the soul and less of the body, my answer is that the same God who made the soul made the body also . . . I maintain that God is worshipped, not only by the spiritual, but by the material creation . . . Our bodies, the temples of the Holy Ghost, ought not to be corrupted by preventable disease, degraded by avoidable filth and disabled for His service by unnecessary suffering.' And though Shaftesbury is here speaking of the care of the Church for its own members, his legislative and philanthropic record exhibit the same care for the world as he showed for the Church.

We have been told that we have in us the power to preserve society from evil, that we are the salt of the earth; so it is our duty not only to pray but also to act. If we do not act, if 'the salt have lost its savour, wherewith shall it be salted?' (Matt. 5:13). The question is unanswered. There is no alternative; the responsibility is ours alone.

28

Salt is the great preserver against corruption, and the Church on earth is here to preserve society against 'the corruption which is in the world through lust'. Corruption not only produces disease and famine, it breaks down all order and stability in society. The evidence of this is everywhere in the world around us today. At one point in the summer of 1967 there were seven areas of fighting around the world, South Vietnam, Aden, Yemen, Suez, North-East Congo, Nigeria and Hong Kong. Most of these were completely unconnected with each other. Most of them arose simply from the hatred of one race of men for another and most of them were disrupting the society in which they were being fought. Later in the same summer there were the terrible race riots in America. Our Lord said that there would always be 'wars and rumours of wars', and only man in his arrogance thinks that he can dispose of war for ever simply by the exercise of his own initiative and intelligence. The evils of hate and suspicion need to be countered by more than human power.

But even without war, corruption strikes at the heart of the society man has organised. This age has been called many things but I, myself, would call it the 'age of indiscipline'. It seems to be taken for granted today that there is some massive cornucopia, some great industrial machine which will pour out to men the benefit of human science while they make less and less effort to obtain it. Today the newspapers are filled with pictures of people who have decided to drop all their responsibilities to society. They ask not, 'What can I contribute?' but 'What can I experience? What new sensual pleasure can I enjoy?'

This was to be the great century of science, the century in which man was at last to conquer his environment, in which power and light would be available to all, in which fertilisers would multiply food production and in which drugs would go a very long way to abolish disease. Hard work, discipline and restraint on the part of a minority of mankind has brought us nearer to these goals. But the corruption of mankind turns every discovery which can be to his benefit also to his destruction. Drugs, which can save a man's body and his reason are being used wantonly and selfishly to destroy the bodies and minds of the weak-willed. Yet those who should be giving the moral lead to society, those who should warn the weak-willed, foolish and simple-minded have fixed as their standard of behaviour the wholly inadequate and changing standard of happiness and convenience, and they have nothing to say and no warnings to give. So the weak use the opportunities of the scientific age to retire into an artificially created world of dream and illusion. Scientific humanism has no power to bring discipline to an age of no discipline, to stop men in the head-long search for sensual pleasure. It has no power to stand against the passion of race hatred. Nor do the Churches have this power if they base themselves on the gospel of scientific humanism instead of the power of the gospel of Jesus Christ.

But it is not only the more obvious evils which produce corruption in the world today. Perhaps the greatest barriers throughout the world to the conquest of poverty and disease are the rather less obvious sins of indolence and avarice.

Those countries which have had the benefit of the Christian Gospel since the Reformation and of some Christian back-ground before that, have had the discipline of the Puritan traditions established in their industrial and commercial life. In Holland, in Switzerland, in Scotland, in England and New England, in Brandenburg and the other countries of the Puritan tradition, generation after generation were taught the Christian duty to work, and in the great commercial centres the merchants were taught the principle that they must not be 'too greedy', that their bargains must be moderate and reasonable and satisfactory to both parties. They were taught to be honest and to honour their commitments. The scientific method owed a great deal to Christians, because they believed that a God of order, a God of reason, a God of unchanging decrees had created a universe whose laws would be in accordance with His nature, orderly, reasonable and unchangeable. It was this belief in the Christian God as the prime cause which banished heathen magic and helped to found the scientific revolution.

The duty to work, avoidance of conspicuous consumption, the honouring of contracts, the scientific method, these are the disciplines on which the Industrial Revolution was founded. These are the disciplines which many of these same countries are now in danger of throwing away. They do not realise what they are losing, and seem to imagine that without Christian principles, life will go on much as before. But if the Christian-based ethic is lost then the dominance they take for granted will be lost also. There is no greater arrogance than to assume that the economic primacy of the industrial West is based on race. It is based on the common heritage of Christian virtues and if these are lost, then the advanced economies and the power that goes with them, will be lost too.

As against the indiscipline, the sensuality, the passion, the indolence and the avarice of the world, what are the virtues of the Christian which help to keep and preserve society? First of all is the simple duty to work. The Apostle Paul has told us 'If any man do not work, neither shall he eat.' But this goes deeper than Paul's simple statement. The Christian believes that man was made in the image of God, that God has given the world to him to develop, that he has gifts which he must use to create more than he was originally given. He must, before he leaves this earth, add to the sum total of human wisdom and knowledge. Our Lord in the parable of the talents made it clear that we are entrusted, each one of us, with talents; that He expects us to add to those talents and that simply to return to Him the talent which He originally gave us is a serious failure of duty. The Christian, therefore, does not regard his life on earth as simply a means of earning a living, of putting in just what is needed to meet his wants and no more. Still less, does he believe that the world owes him a living. He must try to leave the world a better place than he found it. He has got to create something to help society which was not there before.

But not only must he work, not only must he create, he must inspire trust in others, for most work is not done alone. In the great industrial machine we have created men must work in teams; they have to get on with one another, to work together even if they do not like each other. They must be able to trust one another with their money and their careers. But in a world where men care more and more about themselves and less and less about others, where there is less trust and less discipline, the integrity and uprightness of the Christian is more vitally needed than ever before.

The problems of this age are not technical. The theoretical progress which mankind could make from its academic heritage is far ahead of its actual achievement. And what can be done in theory draws away every day further and faster from what can be done in practice. If you look at the economy of any country and you begin to probe the reasons for slow progress; if you try to find why personal income instead of rising at ten per cent per annum rises only at four or two per cent or not at all, then you very quickly discover that the reasons are not technical but human. People say they will not work harder unless they get more money first. Businessmen say they will not invest their money in modern equipment because the risks and uncertainties are too great. They do not trust society sufficiently to be sure that they will be rewarded for their risk. Barriers to trade prevent the spread of new inventions. To all these problems men's only answers are to attempt to apply authoritarian control or to draw heavily upon the remaining effects of Christian teaching — though too often cynicism sets in and no one bothers to find an answer. But human government, however authoritarian, can never succeed in imposing creative activity. Creative activity comes from within man and you cannot make him do it by order of government. You can make a man push a button and pull a lever so many hours each day but you cannot force him to find a better way of doing that job if he doesn't want to. So, without individual trust, restraint and creative work, there is no hope of progress.

The Christian does not have to do anything dramatic to be the salt of the earth, the preservative of human society. He does not have to be a whirlwind of activity. All that God requires is that each Christian does his duty as God has shown him. Provided that we do what is right, what Christian doctrine teaches, God in His power and wisdom will do the rest. It is, of course, no mean thing to do one's duty. It might be easier if everyone else were doing their duty too. But if the Christian acts as the salt of the earth, as the preserver of society,

it is because he is doing his duty when others are not. This often
isolates him so that he stands out as an example and a rebuke.
Because of the hostility this arouses, some Christians will,
inevitably, be crushed. The pages of history are littered with the
stories of Christians who have done their duty and have
suffered for it. But they have not suffered in vain, for suffering
leaves a mark and has an effect. The world is not without a
conscience. It knows, in its heart, what is right and what is
wrong. Paul has pointed out in Romans that it knows the law
because all of us condemn others when they break the law. So
the individual Christian's courage in doing his duty has an
effect on men's consciences and on their behaviour however
hostile they may be. But Christians do not act alone as individuals. Indeed Christians are told that they must band together
with other Christians. They are part of the body of Christ. Their
collective action has an even more inspiring effect than their
individual action and in this way each tiny grain of salt will
have a multiplied effect in preserving the whole area around it.
As the Christian Church grows and increases in a community,
so its effect is felt in ever-widening circles.

Nor is it just the Christian's example which makes the
impact; it is his constancy. Christians have been given a constant and unchanging law. On the other hand, the world
around is inconstant, divided in opinion, shifting and uncertain,
trying one thing one day and another the next. Sometimes one
thing will be in fashion, sometimes another. So that the strong
and constant pattern of Christian behaviour has a strong
polarising effect on behaviour patterns around it, which are
inconstant, contradictory and, therefore, far weaker. The world
can be agreed that it is against Christianity but it is agreed
about nothing else. It can oppose the Christian pattern but it
cannot suggest alternatives. The British humanist, Marghanita
Laski, asked to describe her ideal world, said she found herself
at a loss and that she infinitely preferred to protest against
what she disliked in society than positively to suggest an ideal
for society. The Christian pattern therefore will be the one
which is constant and reliable, the dependable point in an
undependable world. Our work should be dependable. Our

3

friendship should be dependable. Our trust should be secure. Our help should not fail. Our view of life should stand up in death or disaster. The clearer, stronger and more constant Christians become in an inconstant world, the greater the influence they will exercise.

It is only when a Church itself loses faith and courage that influence declines. The world gets tired and gives up easily. The Christian should never get tired and never give up. The world is discouraged but the Christian should have deeper resources and his courage should never fail in the worst adversity. The mind of the world is easily diverted but the Christian never should allow his mind to be diverted from the law and truth of God. This is why the Christian Church conquered the Roman Empire, why it converted the heathen tribes which invaded the Empire, why the Church stood though the Empire fell, and it is why Christian missionaries at enormous peril to themselves have taken the Christian faith throughout the world. To anyone but a Christian the idea that a man should set out for the far ends of the world for a people different in race, colour, language and custom and attempt to win them away from gods whom they and their ancestors had been serving for hundreds, or even thousands of years, and from an age-old pattern of life, would be absolutely ludicrous. But this is what Christian missionaries have done. They say that they have done no more than their duty and that they could not have done otherwise. Sometimes they have had to stay in the same place for years without seeing any results and, long after the man of the world would have abandoned the enterprise as a failure, they have patiently gone on. It is this spirit which has brought the Christian Gospel to every corner of the world so that there are now few countries without a Christian Church. No earthly force has been able to stop the advance of the Gospel of Christ.

As individual Christians facing the power and indifference of the world, we may feel that we are no more than a powerless and despised minority, but we should take courage, for God has given great power to the Church. He has told us, Matthew 18: 18, 'Verily I say unto you, Whatsoever ye shall bind on earth shall be bound in heaven: and whatsoever ye shall loose on earth shall be loosed in heaven' (a verse which Protestants take to mean a general influence rather than a particular ecclesiastical power). He has told us that the Kingdom which He established on earth with a few disciples would grow to a great size. In Matthew 13: 31–32, he said 'The kingdom of heaven is like to a grain of mustard seed, which a man took, and sowed in his field: Which, indeed, is the least of all seeds: but when it is grown, it is the greatest among herbs, and becometh a tree, so that the birds of the air come and lodge in the branches thereof.' The Jews looked upon many of the fowls of the air as unclean (fowls of the air were included among the things which Peter regarded as unclean in his vision at Joppa) and I think that the picture here is of a great Church which houses not only true Christians but also all kinds of outsiders who come to make it their home. Two other parables in the same chapter show the Church as a great institution into which even outsiders will make their way. First, there is the parable of the wheat and the tares, the true believer and the outsider in the same field, then in verse 47 'Again, the kingdom of heaven is like unto a net, that was cast into the sea, and gathered of every kind.'

Many of the problems of the Christian Church are the problems not of failure but success. The fowls that lodge in the branch of the mustard tree, the tares in the field, the bad fishes in the net, are all attracted in because of the size and power of the Church as a human institution. The Church has often attracted people not by its gospel but by its powerful position in the world. The problems of power and success may not be what worries some of us now and may not have seemed a very worrying problem to the persecuted disciples in Judaea, Samaria and Galilee after Our Lord's ascension. It would have seemed to them that the only and overwhelming problem was the bare survival of the Church for the next year—indeed, at times, for the next few weeks. And yet already Our Lord had instructed them on the problems arising from the success and power of the Church as an earthly institution. Later in the Acts of the Apostles and in the Epistles we find already a

Church which has survived the initial persecutions and which is expanding rapidly. For the first time they come up against the institutional problems. Professing Christians come flocking in and some are genuine, but some are not. Those who are not, set about perverting the gospel to make it more amenable to the more worldly life they would like to follow. True, in times of persecution, they leave the Church, but at all other times the shade of the great tree attracts them and they fly in under its protective covering.

In telling us about the impact of the Church on the world, Our Lord did not leave us with these few simple parables. He left us with the great Revelation which He gave to the Apostle John of the underlying factors, forces and powers which would be at work throughout the Church age and which could be a guide, a torch and an encouragement to all God's people in the battles which they had to face. He has not only left us, through the Gospels, the story of His own involvement in the world. He has also left us, through the Revelation a picture of His Church's involvement in the world. He did not remain on the hilltop in communion with God, He was in the middle of the milling mob, helping them, healing them, telling them what was right and condemning what was wrong. The Epistles tell us how to order the Church and how to live a holy life, but Revelation brings us back again to the place of God's Church in this present evil world. It makes clear the way in which those forces of evil work and the way in which we can and must triumph over them. Our Lord was opposed by the false religion of Pharisee and Sadducee. We, too, says the Revelation, will be opposed by false prophets and false religion. Our Lord was crucified by the secular power when it gave its ear to false religion. We, too, may be opposed by secular power when it lends its ear to false religion. The people, like the restless sea, were sometimes for Him and yet at the crisis were utterly fickle and deserted Him in a moment. We, too, will have applause one moment, fierce opposition the next. Yet Our Lord triumphed over evil and so, by His power, will we.

There are people who would postpone the truths in the Book of Revelation to some distant period, people who say that great passages of this book do not and cannot apply to the Church in our own generation or, indeed, to any generation of Christians for the last 2,000 years. I am almost automatically suspicious of any interpretation of the Holy Scriptures which tells me that a large portion of them are irrelevant and that for the purpose of the Christian life which we have to lead, we and twenty centuries of Christianity may as well have been without them. But the book was addressed to churches in John's day so it must have been relevant to them and if the book was relevant to the churches in John's time, surely it must also have a message to Christians in every age.

Revelation is a book of symbols but there is, nevertheless, a clear pattern in the symbolism which, once we find it, shows the message of the book vividly and dramatically.

The story of Revelation is the story of the struggle of the Church against the powers of evil arrayed against it. It is a story told several times over, and what is important to us, in considering the impact of the Christian Church on the world we live in, is that each time it tells of the triumph of the Church and the downfall of its enemies. Whatever the forces of evil may do, the forces of Christ are too strong for them. Not only is there a final triumph and a final judgment but we find a continuing pattern of conflict, of victory for the Church and judgment for the world all the way through the long Church age.

The Revelation is 'The Revelation of Jesus Christ, which God gave unto him, to shew unto his servants things which must shortly come to pass.' The book is not just about the future, 2,000 or 3,000 years after the time it was written, it is about 'things which must shortly come to pass', that is the pattern of life in the Church from Apostolic times onwards. Indeed, the first few chapters are devoted to seven particular churches, which though a pattern of churches in future, actually existed at that time.

The message of God's Word and especially of the Revelation is that the forces of evil are everywhere and, left to themselves, they will possess the field. If nothing is done, the worldly pattern will proceed undisturbed. Worldly religion and worldly government will support one another and will serve the hidden forces of evil. Because they are corrupt, there will be conflict, restlessness, upheaval and decay. Whatever front they present of beauty or order, they are only cut flowers. They have no life power in themselves. But the Church is in the world to confront them. The great message of Revelation is that where it does confront them it will triumph. Whatever the peril, whatever the conflict, the candlestick of that church will remain. But the church which is complacent and does not fight, that is the one whose candlestick will be taken away. The two witnesses of Chapter 11 must set out the law of God and the gospel of Jesus Christ and the law and the gospel have within them the power of transformation of society here and the power of eternal life hereafter.

I believe that it is significant that there are two witnesses. The Christian does not act alone. The man in the pulpit cannot act without the support of the man in the pew. The layman cannot act without the support of the man in the pulpit. The one sets out the doctrine, the other puts it visibly into practice. Faith and works must go together. Words must be seen to lead to deeds. The power of God must be seen in people. There are a thousand theories of life, but only one works. If it cannot be seen to work then the Christian message cannot rise above the rest. It is simply one view among many. But whenever the Christian gospel can produce a body of people who not only denounce evil in all its forms, but can also be seen to rise above it and conquer it in their own lives and can be seen to establish their freedom from all the fetters of evil which bind other men, then its impact and power will be irresistible. God can work directly on men's souls to convict them of sin and evil, but God's normal pattern is to rely on human means and He has made it plain that in the work of conviction and conversion, He depends on every single Christian in His Church.

Each of us has a different calling. Each of us has different problems, different opportunities. Some churches face outright persecution. Others are trying to survive amid civil chaos where the rule of law has disappeared. Some are fighting complacency; but perhaps most today are trying to warn a society which has lost all religious faith that if you empty the soul of error and do not fill it with truth, then seven devils worse than the first will come and fill it for you. The great peril of today is the so-called secular society, facing an irresponsible generation with the useless platitudes of humanism. They remind me a lot of sheep trying to persuade the wolf that they are on his side. But whatever the opposition to the Christian faith, whether it is persecution, chaos, complacency or indifference, the Christian must do his duty and follow God's law. And God's law has been summed up by Our Lord in the two great commandments, 'Thou shalt love the Lord thy God with all thy heart, and with all thy soul, and with all thy mind . . . And the second (commandment) is like unto it, Thou shalt love thy neighbour as thyself. On these two commandments hang all the law and the prophets.' (Matt. 22:37, 39–40.)

For many of us our love for our neighbour will show itself most of all in the way in which we serve the community in our secular work. Every Christian should bring the very highest standards of care to what he does. We should be reliable in an unreliable world, hardworking in an indolent world, responsible and trustworthy in an irresponsible world, careful in a careless world, honest in a dishonest world, inventive and creative in a supine world, a world content to add nothing to human society on its way through life, and in a greedy world, we should be unselfish and restrained. We should still be there to answer the telephone when everyone else has taken time off to watch world cup football or world series baseball. These things, small in themselves, are the tiny grains of preservative salt with which the Christians can help to keep the world from its own corruption.

For others, love for our neighbour will show itself more in our care for those who need help. There is a Christian youth centre in south London to which day after day come all those who have been turned out by society. Their families hated them, the police suspected them on sight, all doors of respectable citizens were bolted and barred against them. At first they hated each other and fought with long sharp knives which never left their sides. Many of them were hooked on drugs. They were the outcasts of a society which condemned them but could not help them. But to the warden of this youth centre they are souls in need. As such she loves them and this love penetrates even their hardened consciences. She was different because she knew them and cared for them each by their name. When a pair of eyes looks through the peephole in the bolted door and sees her on the doorstep, the bolts slide back to let her in. If she thinks they have been picked up by the police just because of their criminal record, she will stand by them and speak for them. But when they are wrong, she tells them so in the firmest possible way. 'The wages of sin is death' is up in large letters on the wall and they understand what it means. When she read Psalm 1 about the 'counsel of the ungodly' and those who sat 'in the seat of the scornful', they knew it was written for them and said so.

Months and years of endless patience and love have had their reward. Knives have been put away, gang fights have stopped, drug addiction has been cured, creative work has started and, above all, there is an increasing interest in, understanding of and response to the Christian gospel. Nothing mattered but that someone cared for them — even for them.

Our Lord was involved in the world and the Church is involved in the world. He did not escape from the world and nor can we. When Our Lord commissioned his disciples to go out to preach, He told them (Matt. 10:24-26) 'the disciple is not above his master, nor the servant above his lord. It is enough for the disciple that he be as his master, and the servant as his lord. If they have called the master of the house Beelzebub, how much more shall they call them of his household? Fear them not therefore . . .' John tells us (I John 4:4) 'Ye are of God, little children, and have overcome them: because greater is he that is in you, than he that is in the world.'

We cannot divorce our Christian belief and theology from personal and corporate practice. We are bound to take sides in the battles of ethics and morals in our own generation. We must be loyal to Our Lord and to His Word in the society in which we live. Only in this way can the Christian act as the salt of the earth.

CHAPTER 4

Church and State

IN WESTERN SOCIETY today the State is for the most part
secular, not committed officially to any religion, pledged to be
neutral between the religious views of all its citizens. This
seems to work, but it is doubtful whether it will work much
longer. Secular States of western society at least are still
drawing very heavily and deeply on the moral capital of
Christianity. All seems well while this goes on. But as soon as
someone calls the bluff, there will be trouble. It would be a
bold man indeed to say that western society had any ideology
as strong and positive as Christianity from which it was
replenishing its moral capital. It would be an even bolder man
who would confidently predict that western society will hold
together without any replenishment. Both Fascist and Communist States established an ideology to back up the power of
the State. In Mohammedan countries the State has a religious
sanction and in many of the ex-colonial States there will be, for
a period at least, some hangover of Christian influence,
though some have very quickly found that tribal loyalty is the
only tie which will bind men. It is interesting that Nkrumah
justified his cult of personality on the need to ride above the
tribal loyalties and found a loyalty to the new State of Ghana.
Liberal theologians may look placidly on the rise of secular
society, may write books to show that this is all part of some
inevitable long-term trend, may try to launch the failing
institutional religion on this new band-waggon; but they have
no justification for seeing today's mixed western society go on
into a rosy future, for believing that such virtues as it has will
remain intact or that these virtues will conquer the Afro-
Asian and Communist worlds. The laws of human nature do
not stand suspended because of technical advance.

There is so little thought today on the relation between

society and the Christian Church, that we have to go back
some way to find a good statement of principle. One of the
classic works on the relation between State and Church are the
chapters in *The Church of Christ* by Dr. James Bannerman, one
of the first professors of New College, Edinburgh. Bannerman
felt that the two societies of Church and State stand so in-
timately and vitally related to each other that the civil magistrate, if he does not ally himself to religion as a friend, will
unavoidably be brought into conflict and collision with it as an
enemy. He felt that the civil element and the religious element
were so bound together in the very constitution of human
society that they could unite together within it as friends but
they could not exist together within it as neutrals. Mutual
tolerance and respect depended on this friendship.

We can never take the tolerance of the State for granted. It is
assumed hopefully that the secular State will always want, on
some general secular principle, to be tolerant of minority views.
But Bannerman felt that it was especially important that the
State should take the Christian view of toleration. He says 'Let
the State be brought to regard man in his relation to God, and
as in matters of conscience responsible to Him; and it will
regard the principle of toleration and the right of private
judgment, in the case of the humblest of its subjects, as a
privilege fenced round with the authority and sacredness of
God. Let the State disown such a view of it, and the principle
of toleration will be deprived of very much both of its security
and of its significance. Any defence of the right of private
judgment in matters of conscience, short of the argument that
it is a right resulting directly from man's responsibility to God,
will, I am persuaded, be a weak and insecure one.'

Toleration is an issue upon which Christians must always be
alert. It does not come naturally to man. It comes with difficulty even to Christians. Protestants had to wait for a century
after the Reformation before the principle became established
and even then they had to fight continually to see that it was
maintained. This fight is still on. It may be that an Oecumenical
movement will be tolerant of all who remain outside it but my
guess is that if it is accorded an official position then there will

be official pressure for conformity to it and the battle for
toleration may have to be fought all over again. For this we
need Christians in the State as well as Christians in the Church.

It can be argued that the State has no power to judge truth
or falsehood in religion; but this is to say that the magistrate —
because he is a magistrate — has ceased to be a man and is
absolved from responsibility to God in matters of religion.
Some argue for toleration on the grounds that all opinion is
innocent when sincerely and conscientiously held. After the
efforts of sincere Nazis in Europe, I do not think that this view
holds much water. Bannerman felt, in any case, that these
arguments put toleration on a level of convenience and that the
right can never be placed on the secure foundation, too solemn
and sacred to be meddled with, unless the State is brought to
see that it is a right of God and not of man. He thought that 'by
divorcing the principle of toleration from its direct relation to
God, it robs it of half its authority, and more than half its
sacredness, and degrades it from the level of a Divine appointment to that of a mere political privilege'. Bannerman felt that
those who argued for a complete divorce between Church and
State would make the Church 'plead with the world for its
heavenly freedom upon the low ground of merely worldly
considerations'. That they 'make the Church of God a suitor to
the world for the freedom which God Himself had given her'.
He pointed out that when Our Lord was at the Bar of Pilate and
called to answer for Himself and His cause and to explain the
nature of His Kingdom and His relations to the civil magistrate,
He vindicated its claims to the protection and toleration of
the State not on the footing of merely political right, but on
the higher ground of divine right. He demanded toleration for
His doctrine because it was the truth of God and protection for
Himself because He was the witness to the truth of God.

Bannerman goes on to point out that if the State is to give
liberty of conscience on secular and not on Christian grounds
then it does not have the safeguards which the Christian
imposes on liberty of conscience. First of all, the Christian's
liberty is limited by the divine law. Conscience, although it is
the supreme law to the individual man, is still under the law

of God. Conscience must also be limited under God's law by the need to maintain civil order in society. Faced with a wave of disruptive protest on grounds of conscience, the secular State has no general principles on which it can base an argument with the protestors. If the protests become too disruptive, it can only resort, in the end, to force, and the toleration it grants in theory comes to an abrupt end in practice. In Germany, Britain and the United States, governments have not known on what grounds they should argue when student protest got out of hand.

Christian freedom of behaviour is also limited by the Church, which can give spiritual interpretation and guidance on issues of conscience in ways not open to the State. Although at the one extreme it is wrong to stretch the authority of the Church so far as to destroy genuine liberty of conscience, yet we cannot at the other extreme stretch the rights of conscience to ignore the guidance of the Church. The Church has a real standing in issues of conscience and this is a genuine safeguard to the State which allows liberty of conscience.

These limits on the rights of conscience are much more severe than the limits which would be agreed by today's secular advocates of freedom of conscience. The hazard to toleration in western society today comes from some secular advocates of individual freedom who are now carrying their claims to such lengths that they could not be granted without danger to the health and structure of society. In Britain recently, a girl involved in a drug case claimed that it was the right of individuals to destroy themselves in whatever way they pleased. The Christian must be seen to be fighting for freedom under a different banner. Otherwise when the inevitable crack-down comes and society rushes to protect itself against disintegration, the baby of Christian toleration will be thrown out with the bath-water of secular licence.

But we must recognise that there are strong arguments in favour of the secular State. The Christian faith is not the only religion today even in Western States. The strongest argument for the secular State is that it is neutral between different religious groups and indeed between the religious and non-religious.

Any State with a high proportion of immigrants will, whatever the moral basis of its civil code, have to decide the extent to which minority groups can be allowed to opt out of this common code of morality. A State whose ethos has been Christian may find itself, as the United States has found itself, with an enormous Jewish population. An appeal to Christian principles will no longer be sufficient as the moral basis of a civil code. Should the State at this point abandon an appeal to Christian principles and appeal to some general secular principles or should it seek an explicit reconciliation between Christian and Jewish traditions? Both Christian and Jew recognise the Old Testament so a very large measure of reconciliation should be possible.

In many Western countries the issue which opens up the Church-State controversy is religious education in schools. Most parents seem to feel that it is right that their children should be given some religious education. They do not want their children to be brought up without morality even if they themselves do not go to church. The United States with its very mixed population forbids all religious education in its public schools. Canada, I understand, has religious education in its public schools with most Catholic children going to private schools. Britain has compulsory religious education but since there are not enough Christians to give it, teaching often falls into the hands of those who do not believe a word of what they are teaching, or worse still it falls into the hands of those professing Christianity but 'denying the power thereof' whose religious teaching is for that reason worse than useless.

Yet another great issue is the extent to which the State should enforce legal penalties for acts which citizens agree to be morally wrong. The most spectacular example of this issue is the attempt in the United States after World War I to prohibit the sale of alcoholic drink. In Britain we have lately tried to lay down legally binding criteria for wage and price increases. In the opposite direction, we have relaxed the laws on gambling as being legally unenforceable and instead of the relatively harmless 'bookies' runner' we now apparently have brought to our shores a fair share of the world's population of criminal gamblers.

Then there are of course problems from time to time as to who is the State. A Christian may have to choose between a State within a Federation and the Federal authority. Or he may have to choose between two powers both claiming to represent the State. Oliver Cromwell, William the Silent, William of Orange, Henry of Navarre the French Huguenot leader, and George Washington all faced this problem. Christians in Southern Rhodesia today have two claims made upon their allegiance. This problem can arise suddenly and unexpectedly and we need to know the principles on which we should make our decisions.

Finally, there are what we in Britain today might call mini-powers, the corporation and the trade union. I have heard people allege that these two mini-powers can be included as 'powers that be' which are ordained of God and that if we belong to them in any way they have some divinely-based claim upon our allegiance. If this is true, then it could have some dramatic consequence but if it is not true then we must know why.

These are some of the practical problems which arise from a Church-State relationship and unless we have our principles right, we will find ourselves in trouble and maybe, since these issues when they arise are key issues, in very deep trouble.

If the Christian is to play a major part in the affairs of the world then he cannot avoid these problems and it is vital that his view of the relationship between the two great divine institutions of Church and State should be absolutely clear. Much of the trouble between Church and State has arisen from false views on their proper relation. There have been those who believe that the Church is part of the State and that the Ministers of the Church are, in fact, officials of the State. This is commonly known as the Erastian view and is held today by Anglicans in Britain and by Lutherans in Scandinavia. There are those who believe the Church to be supreme and the State to be in a subsidiary position. This, throughout the Middle Ages, was the Catholic view. There are those who believe that the Church and State should be absolutely separate and have nothing to do with each other at all. This was the view taken

after the Reformation by the Anabaptists and it is possibly the
predominant view now in America. Finally, there are those
who believe that the Church and State while separate and
distinct should have friendly relations and should indeed at
times be in alliance. They believe that there is 'a groundwork
laid in the nature and functions of the two societies for an
amicable and harmonious co-operation between them, without
confounding the two, or making the one subordinate to or
dependent on the other'. This was Bannerman's view, the view
of the Free Church in Scotland, the view which held that the
Christian Church and the civil State are essentially different
and rightfully independent of one another.

First, he says, the State and the Church are essentially different in their origin. The State owes its origin to God, the
universal Sovereign and Ruler. The Church, as the visible
society of professing Christians in the world, owes its origin to
Christ as mediator. The civil government is an ordinance of
God intended for human society as found in all nations whether
predominantly Christian or not. But the Church as an ordinance
of Christ is founded in grace and is restricted in its jurisdiction
to those who profess the Christian faith.

Secondly, the State and Church were instituted for different
objects. The State has been ordained by God to promote and
secure the outward order and good of human society. Without
civil order or government in some shape or other human
society could not exist at all. But the Church has been instituted
by God to advance and uphold the work of God's grace on the
earth and to promote the spiritual interests of the Christian
community. The one is meant primarily to serve the temporal
good of man, the other to advance man's spiritual well-being.

Thirdly, the Church and State have two separate kinds of
power committed to them by God. The civil government has
the power of coercion to protect the citizen and to punish the
wrong-doer. It has the power of the sword, the right, for limited
number of crimes, even to take life. The Church, on the other
hand, has been given the power of the Spirit, the force of truth,
the light of saving grace, and the influence of spiritual authority.
The Church claims no right over the persons or property of

men but only appeals to their hearts and consciences. It has the right to use instruction, admonition, reproof and censure. It has the right to excommunicate from the body of the Church but having done all that, its power is exhausted. The power of the Church and the power of the State cannot and should not be interchanged.

Fourthly, the State and Church have different administrations. The office-bearers of the State have no official standing within the Church and the office-bearers of the Church have no official standing within the State.

Bannerman believed that 'These two institutions, of the Church and State, equally of Divine appointment have a separate existence, a distinct character, and an independent authority; and that it is impossible to identify them, or to make the one dependent on the other.'

The Erastian view, by contrast, is that the office-bearers in the Church are merely instructors, or preachers of the Word, without any power or right to rule, except what they derive from the civil magistrate. They say that it is inconsistent with the very idea of civil society to permit another and independent society within it. They dislike the idea of what they call an *imperium in imperio* and say that the State cannot stand if another body is to exercise a separate and not subordinate jurisdiction within its very heart. The answer of Bannerman to this is that if the nature of the authority exercised by each is wholly and fundamentally unlike, they can exist together.

According to Bannerman, the Catholic position is laid out in the third Canon of the fourth Council of Lateran which says 'Let the secular powers whatever offices they hold be induced and admonished and if need be compelled by ecclesiastical censure.' It also gives to the Supreme Pontiff the power to declare that a heretic's subjects are absolved from their allegiance. Bannerman quotes Bellarmine as saying 'The Pope has, in order to spiritual good, the supreme power to dispose of the temporal affairs of all Christians.' The world has, of course, changed a great deal since these words were written and in a very great many countries Catholics are now a minority religion protected by the laws for toleration of religion laid down by the secular State. It may therefore be somewhat unfair to hold this out as being the present position of the Catholic Church and there are many Catholic countries — countries where the Catholic Church is the majority religion — where this power is certainly not claimed by the Catholic hierarchy today.

The issues today are in most cases no longer the conflict between an Erastian and a Catholic view of the State. The Erastian position is maintained only in England and Scandinavia and there are many Christians within the Church of England who would gladly see the end of the subservience of the Church to the State. The arguments today are whether there should be any formal association between Church and State or any interest by Christians in the affairs of State. The Erastian position will only become important again if the Oecumenical movement leads to recognition of Oecumenical Councils as the official spokesmen for all religions within the State.

Luther, Zwingli and Calvin all maintained the necessity of a connection between Church and State. Those who did not were considered extremists, especially after the Peasants' War in Germany. But in the seventeenth century the religious wars had done such damage that Christians began to feel for a less rigid identification of the interests of Church and State. In Britain it was Cromwell who, when he had defeated the Erastian party in England and the Presbyterian party in both England and Scotland, first introduced the concept of religious liberty. He not only gave liberty among Christians but also admitted Jews to England for the first time for many centuries. His message to the Scottish Presbyterians is a classic. He said 'I beseech you, in the bowels of Christ, think it possible you may be mistaken.' After Cromwell's death, Charles II and his brother James II attempted to turn the clock back but they were not successful and James II lost his crown in the revolution of 1688 to the Protestant champion William of Orange. In America, the New England Puritans attempted for a time to impose religious conformity but the rapid growth of the American colonies made this impossible and the United States of America was founded as a secular State. The French Revolution of 1789 turned

4

France into a secular State and most countries are now secular States. Since the Protestant and Catholic states of Germany federated in 1870, the British and Scandinavian monarchies are almost alone in having an official State religion.

We have gone a long way today from the reformers' view of the need for a close alliance of Church and State. Zwingli had thought that Church and State belong together as naturally as soul and body. He believed this so strongly that he was quite prepared to fight for his belief and indeed he died in battle not far from Zurich. He had a strong influence on John Calvin who was the greatest exponent of the view although he never defined the nature of the State or systematised his ideas. He believed that both Church and State were ordained by God and for practical purposes he regarded them as one. Anyone who wanted to be a citizen of Geneva should make a profession of faith in Christ. To him, Geneva was a Church. He believed that the State must make sure that the right doctrine was maintained and that sin against God's law must be punished. He believed therefore that the State must conform its laws to the divine laws and that it was the duty of every man to submit to the sovereignty of the State. He believed that the State must help to Christianise the world and therefore brought in by the back door the idea of using the State to propagate the Church's ideas. He had a profound influence on England, Scotland and Holland. The Presbyterian Church followed him and the passage on magistrates in the Belgic Confession is influenced by Calvin's view.

But the view of the reformers tended, in the upheavals following the Reformation, to lead to civil strife, and has been almost completely overthrown. It would be wrong to blame the resulting struggles on the doctrine of the reformers. The Reformation altered power relationships within and between countries and struggle was inevitable. All we can say is that the doctrine of the reformers on Church and State did not give the guidance needed to deal with the vast variety of problems which arose. Therefore they do not give us the solid guidance that we can look for on so many other matters of doctrine.

I believe that this generation has got to find its own relation between the Christian Church and the State. What makes this specially important is the growth of the Oecumenical movement which could open a completely new chapter in Church-State relations. At present we have many varied branches of the Christian Church and of non-Christian Churches in a secular State. So there is no officially recognised spiritual power. This has enabled the Church to take the old Anabaptist position and ignore the problem completely. But there is a constant temptation on the part of Church leaders to try to obtain an official position in the State. A Church which has lost the power and authority which comes from spiritual teaching feels itself bereft and hankers for a position of authority in the community. Some kind of official recognition might go a long way to restore its status. The State, on its side, always needs to consolidate interest groups into bodies with which they can conveniently deal. It is part of the business of government to try to obtain a consensus and its normal mechanism is to get the interested parties together into the kind of official groups which can conduct a dialogue with the government. When the government legislates, it then points to its consultations in support of the legislation it has produced. Its object is to make the consultation sufficiently wide to enable it to ignore the residue of objectors. If the Oecumenical movement does aim to bring a return of official religion the many Christians, who cannot accept the lowest common denominator of Oecumenical doctrine and do not want to be shouldered into the position of residual objectors, can no longer afford to ignore the problem.

What then are the foundations of the relationship between Church and State? Bannerman felt that the one fundamental condition essential to good relations between Church and State and to an alliance between them for common objectives was that each should recognise the other as an independent and distinct body in their entire office and function. The State must recognise that the Church has a right from her Divine Head to the full possession and free use of all the powers which He has vested in her without interference or obstruction of any kind from the civil magistrate. The Church has also a right to expect from the State a legal recognition of her character,

powers and freedom as a Church. The Church must recognise
that the administration of the civil powers and offices shall be
free from encroachment or opposition from the Church, and
the State has a right to expect that the spiritual society shall not
interfere with or hinder the authority and freedom which God
has given to the civil powers as His ordinance for good.

Bannerman felt that if each respected the integrity of the
other there was a foundation for a friendly alliance between
Church and State in the twofold character which Christ
sustains as Head of the Church and also as Head over all things
to the Church. In Ephesians 5: 23 Paul tells us that 'Christ is
the head of the Church'. And in Colossians 2: 10 he says that
Christ is 'the head of all principality and power'. If Christ is the
head over all things then civil government of nations may be
instrumental in advancing the interests and in promoting the
well-being of the Church. We know from the Old Testament
that even where the State is evil God can use it to help the
Church. And with all the hesitation we must have in attributing
events today to the providential intervention of God it is clear
to Christians from time to time that God is using the 'powers
that be' as their providential protection.

On a more practical level Bannerman believed that there was
a foundation for a friendly relationship between Church and
State in the fact that they had certain important ends in common. He pointed out that in addition to man's duty to God
there was a large class of duties between man and man which
it was the joint province of both the Church and the State to
promote. Although the commands of the first table of the moral
law, for example 'Thou shalt have no other gods before me',
are in most senses spiritual, the duties of the second table of the
moral law, such as 'Thou shalt not kill' and 'Thou shalt not
steal', are the concern of the State as much as of the Church.
The duty to respect life, the ordinance of marriage with its
rights and privileges both civil and sacred, the property of man
with the laws which regulate its possession, the duty and
solemnity of an oath, which is part of the cement of society,
the obligation of honesty and justice between man and man are
all concerns of both State and Church.

In a nominally Christian State the Church and State would consist of the same individuals. A Church member taking civil office remains a Church member. Unless we say, as some of course today, that the duties and offices of the State are unlawful to a Christian, there must be some way or other in which the two can be discharged in harmony, some way therefore for the Church and State to live in harmony.

Bannerman points out that under the Jewish economy there was a close and intimate union between Church and State. He does not accept that the Church and State of the Jews were merged with each other but maintains that they still remained separate and independent. He says that 'unless it can be proved that the Jewish Church was no Church at all and that the Jewish State was no State, the fact of the union between them under the express appointment of God cannot be got rid of.' We are a bit inclined today to think of the Jewish State as being a theocracy and therefore not applicable as an example for us today. But even in ancient Israel there was a separation of Church and State. Moses was the law-giver and ruler, Aaron the priest. Samuel condemned Saul for intruding into the priest's office and in the kingdom which followed offices of king and priest were always kept separate. A good king would preserve the true religion but he would not administer it.

Bannerman did not believe in a secular State. He believed that the body politic had a distinct moral personality, capable of right and wrong, and directly accountable therefore to God. He felt that instead of being diminished or cancelled, a man's responsibility as a Christian was increased by the additional obligations he took in his character as a citizen. He denied the view that the State, as a State, had nothing to do with religion or that it was bound to maintain neutrality between the profession and denial of Christianity. He thought that the State had a duty to recognise the true religion and to promote its interests. He believed that there was an intimate and indissoluble connection between the interests of civil society and the interests of true religion and that to promote the well-being or even to ensure the existence of the State it was necessary for the State to call in the aid of powers and influences which it did not itself have. He felt that for the State to dismiss as a matter foreign to it the religious instruction and spiritual well-being of the people at large was to forgo a major instrument which God had put in its hands for securing the authority of law, promoting the ends of civil government and protecting the rights and peace of society. Without some religion no society on earth could exist at all and without the true religion no society could exist happily. Law could not be enforced if it had to trust for its authority on punishment alone, without any higher motive to secure obedience to it, and justice could not be carried out if it had no hold on the conscience and moral sense of the nation. Religion was the only sanction sufficient to enforce right and to deter from wrong in the community, the only bond that could bind together the discordant elements of human society and give peace between man and man.

This view may have been correct for nineteenth-century Scotland, where Christianity was the established religion of a country where most people were still nominal Christians and in similar circumstances, perhaps, the Christian should contend for it as Bannerman did. But it would be contrary to a Christian's belief in toleration to impose his views forcibly on others and a mechanical and unsympathetic propagation of this view would be quite wrong in multi-religious countries such as India or Japan. On the other hand it is no part of Christian toleration to pretend that God's law is not binding on all men. If we have to concede that on particular issues it shall not be the basis of the civil code of the country in which we are citizens, this should be because we must concede to others their right to be mistaken and not because we think that the Christian view is mistaken. Moses did not grant the right of divorce because he thought it right but because the Children of Israel wanted to put away their wives and the wives had to be protected by properly regularised proceedings.

There are no final solutions, only a constant process of argument and adjustment; but the Christian must be prepared to take his place, as a citizen, in this argument and must know the Christian principles on which his own position should be based.

CHAPTER 5

Industrial Society

I SUPPOSE THAT at the beginning of this century most men lived in agricultural societies. There might be some industry in large towns but most towns were not all that large and the predominant pattern of society was agricultural. Even where it was not agricultural it was 'small town' and relatively simple. Now, only fifty years later, the pattern in the Western world is quite different from what it has ever been in the world up to this century. It is only reasonable therefore for men to ask whether industrialisation and push-button nuclear warfare create problems which cannot be answered by a book like the Bible written by men who only knew a simple agrarian society.

First of all we have to ask ourselves just what industrial society is. What is it that has changed and is the change likely to go on within industrial societies; is it likely to extend to agrarian societies?

Industrialisation has produced a tremendous change in the whole pattern of society; and I believe that it is likely to produce even further changes and that it is certainly likely to extend across the world. This change in society has produced a great challenge to Christian Churches and one which has really thrown us back on our own resources, because we can no longer depend on the old institutions and patterns. Industrialisation is an enormous technical breakthrough in the means of production and of communication. 'Breakthrough' is a much abused word today but I use it in the original and genuine meaning. This breakthrough has brought industrial society well beyond the poverty line and has made the average man freer economically than ever he has been before. It has liberated men from the need to earn a living in the confines of the society in which they were born. The continuous expansion, the high employment rates and the high rate of pay for unskilled and semi-skilled jobs mean that a man can pick up a job and earn a living wherever he finds himself. So, for the most part, can a woman and a teenager. Industrial society has not only produced more goods, it has also opened up communications as never before. Men are no longer confined to picking up their ideas from those within a fifty-mile radius of their home. They can travel cheaply for hundreds and thousands of miles. The freedom to earn your money anywhere and the ability to travel almost anywhere have had the effect of an enormous explosion tearing apart a society which has been held together by the constraints of economic life since time began. Against the tidal force of this explosion previous waves of emigration look like tiny ripples. Any boy still tied to his mother's apron strings is there from choice and not from necessity.

Internationally, industrial power has given great military power to the stronger States and it has therefore relatively weakened the weaker States. This shift in the balance of power has been masked to some extent by conflict between the great powers. It only became evident in full force in periods of great power accord. But agreement between the great powers at the turn of the century resulted in the carving up of Africa between them; the balance of power after the First World War, when Russia, Germany and Austria had been defeated and America had retreated into isolationism, enabled the relatively small industrial power of Britain to rule the largest empire the world has ever known. On occasions since the Second World War when the two super industrial powers have had a common policy, nothing has been able to stand in their way. Similarly, within States, the control of the machinery of government and of the armed forces has given enormous power to those who possessed it and has made opposition to them much more difficult.

Industrial society has set up new centres of authority within States. We have had the rise to relative power of organised labour which, when it withdraws labour, can totally disrupt the community. We have also had the rise to power of the great corporations whose revenue can easily equal the revenue of the State. A corporation can dominate a community and some are even big enough to dominate the States whose revenue they provide. Decisions made by Unilever, Shell and Phillips Electric are clearly vital to the well-being of the Dutch State. The decisions of a few aluminium companies are vital to the economy of Norway and of course the decisions of one great corporation may make or break the economy of a small developing State in Africa or Asia.

The increasing dependence of society on its industry and its infrastructure of power and communications gives enormous power of blackmail to a relatively small number of people, both within a country and between countries. This forces a high degree of interdependence within countries and between countries. When there is a strike which affects a whole industry the powers of the State are brought into play until it is settled. What men do at one end of the country is no longer a matter of indifference at the other end. As world trade builds up between countries, so they become more dependent on each other. Tariff barriers between industrial countries are being lowered continuously to get the maximum economies from international specialisation. But this throws burdens on international co-operation which were unknown to diplomats of previous generations. Highly skilled teams of negotiators argue night and day holding out for concessions until the last possible moment and finally when the last possible moment has passed, going through the now well-known procedure of 'putting back the clock' to get a final settlement.

Economic nationalism is discredited. International co-operation by common markets, free trade areas, the General Agreement on Tariffs and Trade, is agreed to be in everyone's best interest. Developing countries may try to raise tariffs to protect infant industries to obtain a broader and more self-sufficient base for their economy but they are going against the tide. Since this increases their industrial costs the process cannot be tremendously significant. This increase in international trade and internal dependence puts a greater strain on the relationship of man with man and nation with nation and if that relationship cracks under the strain, then the consequences are more far-reaching than ever before. In the old days what happened in America did not much affect Europe and what happened in Europe might not much affect America (there were great exceptions like the effect of the American Civil War on the Lancashire cotton trade, though these were really precursors of the industrial society) but today, as the saying goes, if America sneezes Europe catches cold. If economic activity in the industrial West drops so does the copper price and this has a dramatic effect on the economies of Zambia and Chile. This interdependence places tremendous responsibility on the shoulders of the leaders, industrial and political, of the industrial countries and especially of the major industrial powers.

For all these reasons industrial society depends far more than any other society before on the moral qualities of its members and especially its leaders. Industrial society, because it liberates men from previous constraints without creating its own moral principles to take the place of those constraints, is potentially enormously disruptive of social cohesion and disruptive too of any religious institutions which are socially and not spiritually based. But although industrial society appears to be a technical and not a moral phenomenon, it can be argued that it has come into being as a result of the strong moral principles of the men who made the original breakthrough. At a point of time in the Christian, and mainly Protestant nations, the capital accumulation for industrial growth came when enough men decided to work long after the economic necessity for work had passed and they decided to save their surplus and not to consume it in ostentatious expenditure. Many factors contributed to the industrial revolution, but the contribution to the scientific method by men who believed in a rational Creator and the accumulation of capital by men who felt a divine calling to work and to thrift must both be reckoned important prime causes. Not only did industrial society require abstinence and hard work for the original breakthrough but it increasingly requires efforts of self-discipline while producing such a cornucopia of wealth as to appear to reduce the need for those efforts. Without continuing moral strength it therefore bears in itself the seeds of its own destruction. Gross national production has gone up for a long time in most industrial countries and we tend to extrapolate trends to infinity. But history seems to move in cycles, cycles of growth and then of decline as strength leads to prosperity, prosperity to corruption and corruption to decline. If the great societies of North America and Western Europe, which are at the core of the industrial revolution and of world industrial growth, should choose to work less and if the strain and discipline of human co-operation were to prove too much for human nature, then industrial society could decline as rapidly as it has risen.

Not only do we face the problem of how to keep the dynamic of industrial society despite the increasing strain on self-discipline and on human relations which it imposes, but also the problem of how to set moral standards for the conduct of industrial society in order to retain the cohesion of society against the disruption of purely economic forces. As soon as a teenage boy and girl finish their education, they become at once financially independent of their parents. The tie between parent and child today depends entirely upon force of character and force of habit but is devoid of any further sanction. At that age the children have few financial obligations, they are physically tough and can, if need be, walk out and sleep rough. Where the authority of parents is weak and there is no habit of self-discipline, the result can be an arrogant, foot-loose generation, capable of raising trouble at the least provocation. No longer are they immobile in their own home town, but can get cheap and individual transport from the money they earn. This problem hit America in the forties and Britain in the fifties. It has now spread to such well-disciplined countries as Holland and the Soviet Union. The market economy regards these teenagers as an enormous opportunity, a tremendous new market with a great disposable income. It is not the job of the market mechanism to answer the problem it has created.

It would be wrong, however, to think that the teenage problem came first or stood alone. Industrial society has given far higher wages to father and mother as well. In the old days divorce was not only unacceptable socially, it was also, if the divorced wife were to be maintained, untenable economically for all but the very rich. But today it is possible for a working man to maintain a wife and one or even two ex-wives. Divorce has become economically practical. Even for those who are still married the much stronger possibility of divorce has brought uncertainty and with it insecurity to a relationship which formerly was stable and secure. This has led to enormous emotional instability and a far greater interest than ever before in psychiatry and tranquilising drugs.

Geographical mobility undoubtedly helps industrial efficiency. The industrialist is always anxious for the maximum mobility of labour. He wants the greatest possible flexibility for his operations and the greatest availability of the needed skills in the locations where he needs them. What he wants he can usually pay for. But one result of geographic mobility is the breaking up of the larger family, the shearing off of the wider kinship group from the nuclear family. A man will take his wife and children when he moves his job but he cannot be expected automatically to take his mother-in-law, his father-in-law, his own father and mother or his brothers and sisters. All this great community of grandparents, of uncles, aunts and cousins, of in-laws and their connections disappears to the end of a weekly long-distance telephone call. (It is interesting to see how much this call to the old folks is advertised in American magazines.) In Britain there have been some social investigations into the new towns which have been built since the war. One of the great problems which emerges is the absence of 'mum', the wife's mother to whom she takes all her troubles, who looks after the children while she goes out shopping, who is the security and point of reference for all the growing pains of a new young family. Take mum away and life becomes very bleak, lonely and disoriented. Doctors on both sides of the Atlantic find a much higher incidence of mental breakdown in new towns and in the new estates which are too big to be integrated with the local community. Harlow, Levittown and Brama Lea have their advantages. Even in human terms, the picture is not all black. But it takes more than space, modern architecture and neighbours in the same income-bracket to make a human community.

Even if a family sticks together and even if grandparents are not far away, life in today's enormous urban sprawls lacks social cohesion. It is very difficult to find any sense of local community. People work and sleep in widely different locations. Your friends at work have no idea of your home background and your friends at home have no idea where you work. No one belongs anywhere any more and the symbols of success are increasingly artificial. A local community may have its faults but it does have values other than money. A sense of community, of pride in belonging and of pride in achievement is a cement in society, which is removed by anonymous urban sprawl and a constantly shifting population.

I believe that another element of social disruption is the one-class suburb. This not only has the damaging effect on the Church of making it a one-class Church but it puts strong geographic barriers between class and class. It is, of course, economic to build one class of houses on one estate. It is true in Streetsville, Ontario, in Gravesend, Kent and in Salisbury, Southern Rhodesia. It is economic simply because if you put a high-priced house in a low-priced estate you will not sell the high-priced house for what it cost you to put up. Nor does it pay to put a new estate in among old housing. That estate will stick; it will not sell. Furthermore, it is doubtful if you will get the bank or building society to advance loans on the houses. This is not a job for the market economy. But social needs can be met by tough zoning by a local authority or, since this might kill a smaller local authority's development schemes, by a larger area authority.

Another factor in disruption which is possibly not so important now as it used to be is the loss of religious links caused by mobility. A pastor gets to know his flock and there is some force in this personal connection and in the force of friendship between Church members which may bind a family to a Church. Of course this should not affect a true Christian. But although the Christian may welcome the departure of those who went to church for the wrong reasons and although institutional religion can often be hostile to a true Christian faith, the Church as an institution can have a cohesive power in society. Any damage to this cohesive power by breaking of

Church links when people are taken away by new jobs, is another factor in the process of social disruption.

Not only are there great problems in society as a result of the enormous growth of wealth but there are considerable problems of morality in the administration of industrial life itself. Economic activity is not in itself a moral activity. Of course absence of explicit moral principle in economic activity does not mean that industrial leaders have no moral principles. In fact it becomes more and more difficult for a man to rise to the top of the hierarchy of a large and well-run industrial corporation unless he has the kind of moral principle which commands the respect of all those who have to work with him and for him. But the question which the director of the great company must find decisive is whether a proposition is economic and not whether it is right for society. Often, of course, the two run together. Often, even if there is a conflict, a man of principle will stand out for what is right. But today's presidents, vice-presidents, managing directors live in a tough competitive society and they cannot afford to let economics take second place. In fact, the industrialist will often prefer to be put under an obligation by government because he wants to do what is right and cannot unless his competitors are compelled to do the same. He looks for society to lay down the ground rules under which he and his competitors will all have to operate. This is not so easy as it sounds. To the outsider it looks as if government simply has to legislate and all will be well. But legislation takes time; it has all kinds of unforeseen side effects; it is ponderous and difficult to administer, hard to change if it turns out to have been wrong. So governments have increasingly resorted to voluntary leadership. Both in North America and in Europe wage guide-lines have been used in an attempt to prevent inflationary wage settlements. All this puts a heavy strain on industry-government relations and as heavy a strain on management-union relations. There is a great area somewhere between the strict rule of economics and the strict rule of law where tremendous strides could be made if people are disciplined and responsible. But if men cannot agree unless it is either in their immediate self-interest or they are compelled by law, then we shall all be the poorer. Legislation gives no real relief to the strains which industrial society places on self-discipline and human relations.

But the greatest impoverishment of all would come if people in the nations, which created the original industrial break-through, were to lose the moral principles which enabled them to pull themselves up by their own bootstraps. In *The Christian in Industrial Society* I have put in an Appendix, 'The Weber-Tawney Thesis'. This thesis is roughly that the Christian virtues of thrift and honesty combined with a strong sense of duty to work were responsible for enabling the Protestant countries, in which this ethic had developed, to make the original indus-trial breakthrough and to save enough to invest in the new equipment which made the breakthrough self-sustaining. The thesis has been amended and developed by Christopher Hill, Master of Balliol College, Oxford, and though it has been challenged by Professor Trevor-Roper of Oxford, the case for it seems strong. It is certainly true that there is a very strong and direct correlation over the years between a country's ethic and its economic performance. Though this tends to be obscured by the high growth rate of countries which have been helped by defence pacts, investment and technical aid from other countries which have weakened themselves in the process. I believe that we, and those economically dependent on us, are much more heavily dependent on the Christian ethic for our prosperity than most people would now be prepared to admit. If this is true and if this ethic were finally abandoned or if some alien philosophy came to take its place, then there could well be a catastrophic falling off in the prosperity of the Western world.

There are many forces operating against economic develop-ment. First of all there is graft, which can slow all economic development down to a dead stop. Some day someone should do a really good book on graft. It ranges from the small sum you pay the Secretary to the Minister before you can see him, to the enormous fortunes stacked away by arbitrary rulers. The boldest device is to make a purchase of oil or aircraft, pay for it out of the State's exchequer and then sell the oil or aircraft *en route* to someone else as a private deal, the proceeds to be paid to a numbered bank account in a safe country. Indeed, one South American dictator is said to have been overthrown because the tanks which he summoned to his rescue were loyal enough but he had sold the oil for their bearings and fifty yards out of the barracks the bearings went solid and the tanks stopped in their tracks. That was true poetic justice. One Balkan king is supposed to have sold off a great part of his country's air force before he was finally deposed. But the main effect of all graft is to reduce contracting relationships to a state of complete uncertainty while Ministers and their colleagues squabble over the proceeds of forthcoming bribes, bribes which would eventually have to be paid for out of the taxes imposed on the wretched citizens of the country supposed to benefit by the new investment.

But even honesty is not enough. For economic advance we need saving and saving requires that people consume less than they earn. This requires self-discipline as well as trust in the investing institutions, trust in the direction and management of companies and in the honesty of the currency. This trust is not easily earned and, once lost, is not easily recovered. Every scandal and bankruptcy, every run on the bank keeps savings from the capital market, raises interest rates and slows down the rate of economic progress. Every decision to consume rather than save does the same.

There is also, in the Western world, an increased emphasis on leisure. But the industrial West was built up because people went on working long after they had earned enough for them-selves and for their families. They went on working because they thought it was the right thing to work and the wrong thing to idle. Undoubtedly automation will provide for the needs of North America, if not for the needs of Europe, with far less work than before. But if the North American worker just goes fishing, then the world will be poorer. The only chance of bringing a poverty-stricken continent like India up above the subsistence level and of setting it off on its own self-sustained growth is continued economic activity in the West, on which India and other developing countries depend for their markets and for a continuing high flow of aid.

Another increasing hazard in industry is the lack of discipline which has begun to appear as a specific complaint in some areas and some industries. It may be that the nature of the job is at fault, maybe management too is at fault, but it seems certain that allowing for all this, there is still a growing lack of discipline. Disputes about pay could be dealt with; so could disputes about conditions. But where there are disputes for the sake of disputes simply because people are disputatious, there is no known answer.

The most dramatic cause of disruption, because the most immediately damaging, is war. Twice in this century the great industrial powers have squandered their new-found wealth in attempting to destroy each other. No Christian can believe that there will never be war. We are told to expect 'wars and rumours of wars'. But what we should also expect and what the world should expect from us is that the Christian Church will use all its power and influence against wanton destruction and slaughter. To some Christians the question is a simple one of pacifism but I do not believe that this can be reconciled with the Christian message. We are told that rulers do not bear the sword in vain. There are times when governments are entitled to take life in order to defend life and liberty. I believe that they are as entitled to take life for the protection of their citizens from perils from without as they are to take it in protection against perils from within. There are unjust wars and there are wars caused by folly and misunderstanding on both sides, but there are also just wars, fought in defence of humanity. The destruction by the Nazis of five million Jews was a crime against humanity and the war to end that tyranny was surely just.

But if we do not accept the simple pacifist position then we must go to the trouble of making rules as best we may which should guide Christians who have some responsibility for these momentous decisions. We cannot draw parallels between the kings of Israel and Judah in the Old Testament and the Christian Church in this day and age. No one nation is responsible for the Christian faith and no one nation is the instrument of God for punishing evil. Nevertheless, it is interesting to see that the crucial decision which a king of Israel or of Judah

5

had to make was whether he should go up against another nation or not and it was for guidance in this decision that he approached God in prayer.

The decision a nation must make is whether the circumstances leave one option open, and one only, that it must go to war with another nation. Very often, of course, the fact that a nation is willing to fight means that there is no war. The action of the United States in the Cuban missile crisis was probably one such occasion. No one who was in the United States at the time will ever forget the tension between the time of President Kennedy's speech, declaring the United States' intentions, and the news a day or so later that the Russian missile ships had turned back. What a government needs at a time like this is an electorate which realises the issues at stake and is at the same time both restrained and courageous. But too often the moods of peoples on this kind of occasion have been on the one hand frightened, or on the other hand excitable and jingoistic. Nationalism can give a country cohesion and can give a government the ability to carry unpleasant but necessary measures because of an acute national need.

On the other hand, nationalism can easily become unbalanced and a nation can find its identity at the expense of all those around it. Unbalanced nationalism and racialism are, in this age of mass destruction, capable of wrecking in a few days — or even hours — the complex industrial society which it has taken years of patient effort to build. The generosity of the victors in World War II has obscured the destructiveness of war, but this generosity came from nations with a strong sense of moral purpose. Those conquered by a racialist victor could expect no such generosity or mercy. What nations need if they are to live in harmony is a balance between a helpful and useful sense of national purpose and a wider care for all men everywhere. Charity begins at home but charity does not end at home. In the old days there was a group of States known as Christendom. The concept of Christendom extended across national frontiers. It did not prevent one nation in Christendom fighting another but it did do something to prevent wars *à outrance* and prevent frontiers from becoming the tight constraining bands we know today. The nation-State may be an administrative convenience but the Christian above all men should try to lift men's eyes above their own frontiers. There is a real understanding between Canada, the United States and Britain about many common problems. But this attempt at mutual understanding is the spirit which especially animates the Commonwealth and is important because the Commonwealth is a multi-racial community. I am sure that the Christian who spends his time fostering this kind of international understanding can do nothing but good.

To sum up, I believe that the problems which face industrial society are moral rather than technical and that if we do not find moral answers then all our technical expertise will be useless. It is part of my job to look at the problems of faster economic growth in one country, to try to find out why what can be done in theory is racing away from what is actually applied in practice, so that the gap between theory and practice gets wider and not narrower every day. Time and again the answer to these problems lies in motivation. The problem is whether people want to work or not, whether they are prepared to take risks or not, whether, on a human level, they are able to get on with each other or not, whether they trust each other or not, whether someone somewhere is being too greedy.

There are tremendous jobs for the Christian in our industrial society. We need to see that the enormous potential wealth in the world is tapped; we need to see that it is fairly distributed, that rewards go to those who deserve them, but that there is a proper safety-net to catch those who are unfortunate. We need to restore some cohesion to society in the developed industrial countries and we need to see that the developing countries are given a leg-up so that they too can get on their way. We need to avoid the catastrophic quarrels of war and yet to defend ourselves against tyranny and aggression. And finally we need to ensure that the Christian Church is fully involved in the world around it and that the world is aware of the great, and eternal message of the Christian Church to the individual and to society.

CHAPTER SIX

Personal Involvement

IF THE CHRISTIAN is not to stand off from society, if he is not to be negatively critical of the world around him then how best can he give constructive help? And how can he be involved in the world without being seduced by a way of life which is alien to his faith?

To the Christian who faces non-Christian society from a safe position inside the ramparts of the Church, the non-Christian world may seem to be all of a piece. He reads that 'He that is not for us is against us' and reckons that however friendly the outward appearance of the man of the world, he is at heart hostile to the Christian faith. Some may argue that no Christian is so simple-minded as to see the world in those black and white terms. But there is much Christian teaching which does divide the world into black and white. Luke tells us that Our Lord said (Luke 12:51–53) 'Suppose ye that I am come to give peace on earth? I tell you, Nay; but rather division: for from henceforth there shall be five in one house divided, three against two, and two against three. The father shall be divided against the son, and the son against the father; the mother against the daughter, and the daughter against the mother; the mother in law against her daughter in law, and the daughter in law against her mother in law.' Men do divide from each other on the Christian faith and even the most disarming Christian approach can produce violent reactions from people otherwise full of courtesy and charm.

But having said and admitted all that I am sure that it is quite wrong for the Christian to treat society as if it were uniformly hostile to the Christian faith. No one is without a conscience or some sense of what is right. Workers among even the toughest cases in society find the most unexpected response to Christian teaching. The world is subject to general influence

for good because God's Spirit is still at work; but it is influenced
in particular by the good and the love that it sees in individual
Christians. It is influenced a good deal less by impersonal
propaganda.

Just as the world is not all of a piece, so not all Christians are
called to go into the world in the same way. Not all Christians
have the same strength, wisdom and talent and, just as the world
is subject to influence for good, so Christians are regrettably
subject to influence for evil. As Paul tells the Corinthians
(I Cor. 10:12) 'Let him that thinketh he standeth take heed lest
he fall.' Many a man has gone out in the world to win them to
the Church and has been won to the world instead. We each
need to know our own strengths and weaknesses. Paul told the
Romans (Rom. 12:3) 'I say, through the grace given unto me,
to every man that is among you, not to think of himself more
highly than he ought to think; but to think soberly, according
as God hath dealt to every man the measure of faith.' He then
went on to point out that although we are all members of the
body of Christ we all have different gifts. The encounter between the Christian and the world is subject to numerous
cross-currents and not to simple rules. What is right for one man
is wrong for another. What is right at one time can also be
wrong at another. Nevertheless, there are some basic principles
laid down in the Christian faith and we must try as well as we
can to apply these to our particular case.

First of all, what was Our Lord's example and how far can we
follow it? The first miracle performed by Our Lord was at a
wedding where He turned water into wine. The great complaint which the Pharisees made against Jesus of Nazareth was
that He was a gluttonous man and a wine-bibber. They
complained that He mixed with the social outcasts, the pub-
licans (or Roman tax farmers) and sinners (Matt. 11:19).
We read elsewhere (Mark 12:37) 'and the common people
heard Him gladly'. Our Lord was truly a man of the people.
He not only mixed with them, but He did His best to help
them. He loved them and cared for them and they knew it and
responded.

But together with this involvement with people went the long

hours of silent prayer when He would withdraw from the multitude and find a quiet place on a mountain apart so that He
could pray to His Father in heaven. This was His source of
spiritual strength. Although He lived amongst the people He
never fell into their sins. The Christian, like Our Lord, must be
in the world but not of it. He must be as much involved with
the cares of ordinary folk as Our Lord was and yet he must not
be wholly involved because he has a call to a higher life and a
higher communion which demands his attention and his
energies too. The more we are in the world, the more time we
must spend in prayer and meditation and the closer must be our
communion with God. Yet this is often easier to say than to do.

Paul has set us an example too. When he was a prisoner on
the journey to Rome he might well have ignored the problems
and troubles of that ship. If anyone was entitled to put up a
barrier against the world around it was Paul. He had fought a
good fight, he had played his part in the founding of the
Church and, as he says elsewhere, it was a matter of indifference
to him whether he stayed on earth or went to be with Christ
'which is far better'. His companions were the Roman guards
who would cheerfully have butchered all the prisoners at the
end rather than let them escape, the seamen who would have
deserted the ship and left it to its fate, and a collection of
prisoners from the jails of Palestine. Yet to this hostile and un-
lovable bunch of people he is full of care and advice. At first
they take no notice of him. He advises them to winter where
they are and they ignore him and sail on. Then there is a
terrible storm, but instead of wasting time in recriminations, he
prays and he does not hesitate to tell them of his assurance of
their safety. Nor is he passively content with that assurance. He
finds that the sailors are about to leave the ship and warns the
centurion, who orders his soldiers to cut the ropes of the lifeboat
and keep the sailors on board. Then he makes sure that they all
have a square meal before the boat runs on to the rocks and
finally when they have all scrambled on shore, soaked to the
skin, we find Paul busy lighting a fire. That, to me, is true
Christian involvement.

But with all Paul's involvement he could still warn us that

there was a point beyond which the Christian should not go. He told the Corinthians (II Cor. 6:14–17) 'Be ye not unequally yoked together with unbelievers: for what fellowship hath righteousness with unrighteousness? and what communion hath light with darkness? and what concord hath Christ with Belial? or what part hath he that believeth with an infidel? and what agreement hath the temple of God with idols? For ye are the temple of the living God; as God hath said, I will dwell in them and walk in them; and I will be their God and they shall be my people. Wherefore come out from among them, and be ye separate, saith the Lord, and touch not the unclean thing; and I will receive you.' Paul does not specify what yoke he is talking about. Any kind of partnership is a yoke of sorts; the most permanent and binding is marriage, but some people have extended this passage to cover business partnerships with non-Christians. I do not think we should draw up precise rules since Paul did not do so, but we should have it firmly fixed in our minds that, in any enterprise which involves a close identity of interests and aims, a Christian is best not to pick a partner whose aims and interests must be deeply different from his own.

The Christian, if he is still daunted by the apparent indifference of the world, has to remember that all men are susceptible to the influence of other men. It is part of the constitution of human nature that people respond to the ideas and moods of those around them. This is clearly visible in children but tends to disappear behind the adult's veneer of self-sufficiency. It is an odd thing, but nobody will ever tell you when you have won the argument—indeed some people having won their point without realising it almost lose it again by going on too long! The Bible has some stories of men or women of evil influence, but for the most part it is an account of how God's servants have lived in the world with all its wickedness and have by His help, influenced it for good. Not only is the Bible peopled with followers of God who are also men of affairs, but every century since the founding of the Christian Church has given men in the same mould.

Since each of us has a different calling and since the worlds in which we are involved are so different, we can only give each other general guidance and examples. But our faith does give us some principles to follow in our relations with the world outside the Church.

First of all, I am sure that we should throw our full energy and enthusiasm into whatever secular job it is that we have to do. The layman is not a second-class Christian and his job is not a second-class job. Christians are right to emphasise the role of the Church in evangelisation but they are wrong to believe that evangelisation begins and ends in the pulpit. The man in the pulpit can no more do the job of the layman than the layman can do his. (This unfortunately does not stop a lot of them from trying.) The ordinary Church member is the bridge between the world and the Church. His job takes him into the world and he meets people who do not go to Church or who, if they do go, are no more than nominal in their Christianity. All that most outsiders know about the Christian faith will be the kind of lives which are led by the Christians they happen to know. What impresses them is not what we say but what we do. 'Whatsoever thy hand findeth to do, do it with thy might' (Eccles. 9:10). The Christian should not be the man who makes a mess of his job, who is half-hearted, who does not seem to know why he arrived or where he is going. The Christian faith should give a purpose to life and a good conscience should give a serenity to which the man of the world can never attain. But above all, the Christian should have a sense of duty and a sense of love for others which should make him put more into his job than he gets out of it. The world is very quick to distinguish the passengers in the team from those who carry the load. In industrial society most men now have to work in teams. Even the professional, whose skill used to enable him to work on his own, is now as likely as not to find himself part of an interdependent team of specialists.

The Christian has a duty too to maximise his personal talents. We were made in the image of God the Creator and if we too are to be creative we must leave the world a better place than we found it. It is not enough for the Christian simply to get by, he has got to make an active and positive contribution.

Our Lord tells two very similar parables, the parable of the talents and the parable of the pounds. The one is in Matthew, Chapter 25, and the other in Luke, Chapter 19. The repetition of the theme marks the importance of the story. In the story in Matthew 25 a man gave to his three servants five talents, two and one respectively 'to every man according to his several ability' and left them. 'Then he that had received the five talents went and traded with the same, and made them other five talents. And likewise he that had received two, he also gained other two. But he that had received one went and digged in the earth, and hid his lord's money.' When the lord came back to reckon with them, he commended those who had made use of their talents 'Well done, thou good and faithful servant: thou hast been faithful over a few things, I will make thee ruler over many things: enter thou into the joy of thy lord.' But to the one who had done nothing with his talent 'His lord answered and said unto him, Thou wicked and slothful servant.' Although I have no doubt that these parables apply to spiritual gifts, I am sure that they apply to natural gifts also. There is nothing in the context which confines the parables to spiritual gifts and both parables are actually about the use of earthly resources. The man who made no use of his resources seemed to be under the impression that in husbanding what he had been given he was doing nothing wrong. It is easy to believe that provided we do nothing positively wicked we are being sufficiently virtuous. But these parables make quite clear that each man is given something in trust from God and that to fail to make use of this gift is a sin. It is, of course, a far easier life if we take on a job well within our capacity, if our mind and talent is not under stretch. It is very satisfying, and indeed very peaceful, to do a job well, and to be aware that no one can criticise you for your competence. It is much tougher to take on a job beyond your immediate experience and to be temporarily out of your depth. On the other hand, this has its own kind of satisfaction. It is always much more exciting to be at the limits of your ability, to be trying something new, especially if this is on the frontiers of knowledge itself. The Christian will often find himself biting off a bit more than he can chew.

This is not an exhortation to ambition. The ambitious man is anxious above all for the credit and status. But the Christian's instructions on this are quite clear. Our Lord has told us not to push ourselves forward, but to wait until we are called. The Christian should act as he does without regard to status, position or financial reward. These will probably come, but if they do not it should not make any difference. I am not saying that the Christian should never put in for a rise in salary or negotiate the best salary for a new job, but that these should not be his first considerations. If the Christian makes a real contribution to his team at work he will have gone a long way to making the Christian faith a living reality to that part of the world outside the Church he is most likely to influence. If he fails in action he is unlikely to make up for it by words. If he fails at work, he is hardly likely to succeed elsewhere.

Many a man of the world may well go along with the Christian's philosophy of work up to this point and many a non-Christian will do a job better than his Christian colleague. The Western world still has enough of the old Puritan ethic to make man want to push back the frontiers of knowledge and experience and to do things that have not been done before. But the man of the world will, too often, do this to the neglect of everything else. By definition, he can neglect Church life. He may find time for community activities, though too many do this just because it helps their career and what does not help they will cut out. But it may be that the man of the world will achieve his job performance by neglecting his own family. The Christian must never, never neglect his family. The family is the cement of society, its basic unit, and is one of the few human institutions ordained of God to hold society together. But Christians who have the additional burden of Church work on their shoulders seem just as likely to neglect their families as non-Christians. In England we have a simple and brutal system of sending children away to boarding schools for two-thirds of the year. The polite but distant conversation between a father and son lunching in a London club after three months apart has to be heard to be believed! I remember being shown a women's magazine article by a mother, entitled 'Little

Strangers' advising other mothers how to deal with these periodic disruptions of outsiders into a well-ordered house. But however important our work may seem to be, however pressing outside claims upon our time, our relation with our children is unique. A child has only one father and one mother. Both have their part and if one or both are missing most of the time then that child will have a lopsided existence and will not be brought up as God intended. The Christian's duty is to all men, but first to those of his own household. None of us can guarantee that our children become Christians, but we must pass on to them our understanding of the Christian faith as best we can and make sure that if at any time they turn their backs on the faith it will be in spite of us and not because of us. In an age in which the whole concept of marriage and the family has become debased, the Christian must set an example of family life at its best. Just as the Christian Church makes more of an impact than the individual, so the Christian family, capable of living in close quarters with love, tolerance and respect for each other, will have more impact on the neighbourhood than an individual living on his own. And a man incapable of commanding the respect of his own family is less likely to command respect outside it.

Having done the best we can in our job and for our family I believe that we still ought, if it is at all possible, to take on some responsibility, some involvement, for the community in which we live. It is not enough to be in touch with the world just in order to earn our living, we should make some contribution for free. We are in the same boat as those who live around us. We have common problems which someone has to solve and at the very least we should be seen to be making our contribution to solving them. Today most communities will have a dozen or so worthwhile voluntary organisations doing a key job for the community itself or making an outreach from the community to those in need elsewhere. Of course there is always the danger that we become over-organised to no good purpose, that committees for this and committees for that become no more than seed-beds of gossip. But commonsense should tell us when we are doing a really useful job and when we are not.

What is important is that our care for others, for prisoners, for the sick, the poor, the old, the orphans, the mentally unstable, the disabled, should not be limited to the confines of the Church.

Some Christians may feel that they have a vocation for the wider fields of public service. Public service in most countries has two broad spheres, advisory and political. The adviser, whether a full-time civil servant or part-time member of a commission, can have great influence but he has no final power. In the end someone else has to take the decision and carry the can. He will do background researches, sit on investigatory commissions and on the basic factual data that he and his colleagues produce, the great decisions of the day will be made. To many Christians, this is the ideal form of public service. They do not get involved in the mud-slinging and backbiting of politics, their name is not associated with controversial measures, they do not have to support people they do not approve of or to defend the whole party programme. It is their political masters who take the decisions and the knocks.

Yet just because ultimate power is, in a democracy, in the hands of the elected representatives of the people we should have Christians among those representatives.

Life in politics is rough. After three years in a job in close contact with politicians I still wonder that anyone chooses it as a way of life. It is badly paid, it is subject to termination at short notice, it puts enormous strain on friendship, and power, when it comes, is often a bitter disappointment as cherished schemes are battered and pounded by forces apparently outside the politicians' control. But perhaps the most distressing discovery the new politician makes is the hostility brought on in the most unexpected places by the very act of political allegiance. A British comedian, Jimmy Edwards, famous for his long moustaches, stood for Parliament in 1964. He said that he had faced rough houses and cat-calls before but what he had not reckoned on, and what really worried him, was that every time he got up as a politician half of his audience were against him automatically and on principle. It is sometimes assumed that all politicians are thick-skinned. This is not my experience. And even if the politician may be thick-skinned, his wife and family may not. I remember one junior Minister telling me what a relief it was to have switched jobs. He said that in his previous job he could take the slanderous mail himself but he found it hard to bear the things which were said to his wife and children.

Yet at a crisis of affairs, when some fateful decision has to be made it falls upon the frail shoulders of one of our political leaders. And if those who have the ability to accept this burden fail to do so for purely personal reasons then our country and perhaps others too will be the worse off.

Even if we do not run for office ourselves we can play a very positive part in political life. Political parties are run by a minority of activists. And any politician is grateful if the activists in his party machine are sensible and intelligent people. But just because politics is a rough game, the party activist will too often be a person who can only see one point of view. The wretched politician is then left to bring home the facts of life the best he may to those who can see nothing but a party ideology. Of course to the narrow-minded his own doctrine is always the self-evident truth. It is always the other side who are blinded to the truth by their narrow doctrinaire prejudice. In this atmosphere the dialogue between Parliament or Congress and the grass-roots becomes hypocritical and unreal if it is not to be painful to both sides. This in turn breeds cynicism and distrust mitigated by a few senseless ideological decisions taken as sops to the party faithful. The Christian who, above all men, should ride above sectional prejudice has a real job to do at the grass-roots level as well as in state and federal Parliament.

Politics and public service need idealism but they are not an ideal world. There are temptations and it is not too hard to fall into them. Perhaps the greatest temptation, because the least obvious, is the temptation to keep out of trouble, to be interested mainly in a quiet and dignified life which offends no one and harms no one but, on the other hand, does no one much good. In industry, performance can be precisely measured in the profit and loss account at the end of the year. Risks are worth taking because there is a visible reward and very often the greatest risk of all is to do nothing. A business man is judged not on his actions but on the results of his actions. This is a harsh judgement because there are forces beyond the wit of any one business man to avoid. Many an indifferent business man has ridden the crest of the wave and many a good business man has had to struggle fiercely against the tide to stay where he was. But the public servant and his political chief are judged on the actions they take and only very indirectly on their results. Indeed, the result of action taken in any large-scale enterprise including government is increasingly remote in time from the action taken and such are the intervening cross-currents that it is extremely difficult to pin down cause and effect. Many men today ride on the achievements of their predecessors and leave nothing but problems to their successors. Action of any kind tends to be controversial because it normally involves disagreeable change in the established pattern and those affected by the change can be expected to shout loudest. The temptation to do nothing and to hope for the best must be very strong. It is much easier to lay blame for action than for inaction. The temptation is to do something superficial and showy but not to tackle the real trouble. In public service, the onus is on the man, who wants to make the change, to show why things should not go on as before and the whole training of the public servant is to discover and to point out the difficulties which will arise when changes are made. Proposals for change are examined with the utmost care and rigour. This has the merit that a proposal which survives the cross-examination is usually soundly based, but it also means that the man who wants to get things done has got to have an unusually high degree of purpose and staying power.

The industrial manager, the other kind of leader in industrial society, faces similar problems and also needs the sense of purpose and the patience which the Christian should be specially fitted to contribute. Although the forces of competition will act as a spur to the average industrial manager, it is perhaps his most important duty too to overcome the forces of inertia and use to the full the resources which are under his control. But to get change where change is needed is one of the toughest jobs in industry and only a limited minority of managers do it as well as they should. People are content to administer and to stick to well-trodden paths. Change, even where it is obvious, is made unwillingly and slowly. Any sales-man will tell you how tough it is to sell a new idea. Change means the re-learning of old skills; it means teething troubles; unpredictable problems will arise; labour may stand out against new methods and there may be strikes and disruption of the smooth flow of work. Change may gain new customers but it may also lose old ones. And yet it is on continuous change and improvement in our industrial processes that our economic advance depends and on the economic advance of the greater industrial countries depends, in turn, the advance of the developing nations. The Christian who is an industrial manager has to remember that the well-being of many people depends on his courage in tackling tough decisions and on continuous creative improvement in the job that he does. If we agree that it is part of our task in life to use our creative talents we must not be content passively to administer the innovations of previous generations.

There are other problems which are peculiar to industrial management. Management in today's industrial enterprise has the difficult job of holding a fair balance between labour, capital and the customer. All three make claims upon the enterprise. The semi-autonomous public company, answerable in theory to the shareholders but often in practice to no one but itself, still has to find the ethical guide-lines which will show it how to reconcile these divergent claims. Of course if a company does not pay enough for its labour it will not get any. If it cannot return a profit to its shareholders its supply of finance will dry up and if it cannot give value to its customers it will sooner or later have to close down. These are the ultimate sanctions. But a long way short of these ultimate sanctions managements have to make decisions on prices, on wage claims and on dividend payments. The old axiom was that a business had to maximise its profits, that it should exploit the market for the maximum price and pay the minimum possible

price for supplies and labour regardless of the social consequences. But big business today has gone a long way beyond
those crude and now unworkable rules. Big business operates
to a long time span. Decisions made today will pay off only in
three or four years' time. To exploit today's market for labour
or for the company's goods in the short term would almost
certainly bring retribution in the longer term. So we have
companies which state their objective to be 'maximisation of
profits in the long run'. But what are the maximum profits in
the long run? Indeed, how long is the long run? Other companies therefore state that their objective is simply to remain
in business in the long run. This means that their prices must be
sufficiently competitive to retain their market share against all
comers, that their wage rates must be high enough to retain a
skilled and stable work force, and that their profit record should
be good enough to attract the additional capital they require to
maintain their competitive place in the market.

If we accept this view — and I imagine it is a view which most
enlightened businessmen would accept — then as industrial
managers we will find ourselves making tough bargains with
labour in order to preserve the profitability and price com-
petitiveness of the business, making tough bargains with
customers in order to have enough money to meet the claims of
labour, and raising capital at the keenest possible prices in
order to preserve the future of the enterprise. No Christian
need be ashamed of finding himself a tough negotiator. But his
aim as an industrial manager should be to run his company so
efficiently that he is able to do just that much better for his
workforce, his shareholders and his customers. It is the poorly
managed and inefficient company which is driven to make the
oppressive bargain.

The Christian must have the reputation in the market place
for fairness and honesty, but perhaps the greatest contribution
which the Christian industrial manager can make is in his
relation within the enterprise to those who are in his direct
charge. A professional job may have its personal relationships
but the professional man normally only advises, he does not
control and command other men. The direct charge of other

81

men and their work is one of the greatest responsibilities any man can shoulder. It is here that one's real qualities as a man and as a Christian are put to the test. The Christian should always make certain that he treats his fellow men with respect. The Christian knows nothing of 'the masses'. He only knows individual souls answerable to God for their actions and each separately created by God in the dignity of His image. However far men may have gone from the image of God, however rough or debased they seem, the Christian must never despise them but must always treat them with respect. Our Lord has set us an example in this which we must follow.

The Christian manager must never be arbitrary in key personnel decisions. In hiring, firing, promotion and admonition he should always act carefully and judicially by agreed procedures. He should never in these key judgments act alone, so that he not only does justice but is seen to do justice. One of the best company chairmen I know, with the ablest of minds, who could take the quickest commercial decisions, is always slow and deliberate in any decision involving people. He would forgive his managers a commercial misjudgment but he would not forgive them the mishandling of people in their charge.

The Christian's qualities as a Christian should come out best in his handling of labour relations. The same goes for a Christian who is a union leader. Perhaps the most useful guide to good labour relations is to try to see what it is that the union leaders want from the managers and the managers want from the union leaders. Labour negotiations need courage. Each side to a bargain must have the moral courage to support the bargain to his own side. The manager must do his best to persuade management to support him, and the union leader must do his best to persuade the men to support him. Neither side to a negotiation wants to find himself dealing with an ineffectual opposite number. It is not always enough to try to convince your own side to accept the bargain you have made, but both manager and union leader will need, at some time in their career, to stand by a bargain when their own side is unconvinced, even if it is at the risk of their job. Each side wants to know that the other side is listening to their arguments. I have

6

known cases where an arbitrator to a dispute has found that the management had convinced themselves that the men's case was entirely irrational but had not gone to the trouble of going down to the shop floor to find out what actually went on. Top management can delegate a good many things in a business, but it should never be too remote from the real problems which face the men who work for it.

It is also a good rule of labour relations that bargains will not be struck between management and men at the expense of the rest of the community. We all know the easy bargain where a wage increase is conceded for the sake of peace and passed on in total to the customer. The whole object of the voluntary prices and incomes guide-lines which have been operated both in Britain and in the United States has been to bring moral pressure on management and unions to keep wage increases within the genuine increase in productivity. On the other hand the union knows no way of improving its real standard of living than by claiming an increase in money wages. What it hopes, and indeed has every right to hope, is that the management will make the productivity improvement to see that this increase is real and does not disappear in inflationary price increases. The unions therefore want an employer who will do his very best to increase productivity and to give a fair share of the increased productivity to his labour force.

On the other hand, the employer will want a labour force which will not resist increases in productivity by putting up phoney protective practices as part of a bargaining pressure to exact wage increases higher than the productivity increases. 'Selling the rule book' is a fine idea so long as it does not produce rules which are made simply to be sold.

Both labour and management will be happier if neither side tries to exploit its temporary bargaining strength to the limits. It is especially dangerous for a labour leader to try to exact the last cent out of a tight labour situation. This can only create pressures on employers, and indeed on government too, to produce a state of affairs where the labour market is always easy and men who might work are being kept idle at home. Indeed, it is a great credit to the self-discipline of a country if it can run at full employment without inflationary wage increases and it will be a happy day when the cynics are no longer able to point to the direct relation between the rate of unemployment and the rate of increase in money wages.

Management above all want labour who will be responsible in the leaders which they elect. Nothing is more frustrating for the management than to find that its labour force have light-heartedly elected an irresponsible leader and nothing is a greater relief to management than when a labour force finally sees through someone who has been irresponsible.

Although a work force will sometimes be irresponsible towards a good management, management normally gets the labour it deserves and responsible management normally gets responsible labour. A friend of mine once took a job as labour relations officer in a large company. He listened to the management and their bitter complaints about the irresponsibility of the unions. He listened to the unions and their bitter complaints about the irresponsibility of management and after a brief period he came to the sad conclusion that the company was in trouble because both were right! It may well seem cleverer or more convenient to a management to keep its plans to itself for as long as it can and then to try to rush them through in a crisis mood before anyone realises what has happened; but if full consultation may be a nuisance in the short run, it is almost certainly right in the long run. The key to good management labour relations is mutual trust. This is something that has to be built up over a long period of time by a consistent record of good faith, but which can rapidly be destroyed by irresponsible action on either side. These are only limited examples of the ways in which a Christian can be usefully and constructively involved in today's society. There are many others. Christians have made a tremendous contribution to the professions, to teaching, to medicine, to the law. They can make their contribution through literature and the arts and in many other ways. All we can try to do is to see how Christian involvement might work out in particular cases, but each Christian must work out for himself how he can contribute to society and how he can deal with his own set of problems.

If the individual Christian is to be as deeply involved as he should be in affairs of the world, if he is really to try to make the world a better place, then he will not only need a deeper spiritual life, he will also need the counterpoise of Christian friendship and fellowship to keep his life in balance. We are much more subject to outside influences than we realise and it is all too easy to slip into the habit and pattern of thought of those with whom we work. It is not enough just to go to Church and have a nodding acquaintance with other Christians. Every Christian needs a real friendship with fellow Christians whom he respects, whom he treats at least as equals and whose plain friendly advice he will accept. Too often Christians who have moved ahead in the world feel that they have outgrown their fellow Church members and put themselves into the position where no other Christian will willingly give them advice. The danger is that the Christian who has made his way in the world will not only discount the advice of fellow Christians who have not gone so far, but will also discount the advice of his friends who are not Christians and this leaves him in a peculiarly isolated and vulnerable position. We need friends who believe what we believe, but who will also in the kindest of ways pull us down a peg or two when we are in danger of getting above ourselves.

CHAPTER 7

Christian Ideals for Society

(i) DEMOCRACY

MOST OF US spend so much of our time in complaining about what is wrong with the world around us that we find very little time to sit back and think of the kind of ideal world we should like to have if this were possible. It is much easier to point out what is wrong than to give a complete and consistent pattern of what would be right. It is much easier to right an isolated wrong if you don't have to think of the effect elsewhere of righting it. But if you are actually in the business of government then you know that any action, even righting a wrong, will have side-effects and these side-effects may create other wrongs which are worse than the one which you have righted. So if we are going to set out the Christian's ideals for society we have to make sure that they are balanced ideals, that they are consistent with each other and that we really could live with the consequences. We fight wars to make the world safe for democracy and we denounce the wrongs of imperialism only to find that the newly-founded democracies have in many cases been nothing more than a power vacuum, to be filled in next to no time by military dictatorships. We aim for a more egalitarian society and try to make life safer and more worthwhile for those who are least able to stand on their own feet only to find more and more people willing to live on the initiatives and hard work of others. We advocate principles of toleration only to find that those whose creed is intolerance take advantage of a freedom which, if they were successful, they would immediately take away. In setting out his ideal society the Christian therefore should not only be idealistic, but he should also be realistic. To some extent men will appreciate good when they see it and to that extent his idealism will stand, but to the extent that there are corrosive and destructive forces of wickedness in the world, his ideals must be safeguarded to see that they are not abused. He has to distinguish societies which are solidly based on a Christian consensus and influenced by Christian habits of thought from societies influenced by centuries of pagan religion and lacking in the Christian's respect for the individual.

Most Christians living in democracies would, I think, hold that the only form of government which a Christian can accept as his ideal is democracy. A democratic constitution embodies the respect of the Christian for the individual as someone who is both responsible and answerable for his actions. It is a safeguard against tyranny and against the oppression of the poor by the rich. Where it commands respect it is an efficient means of government, because efficient government requires the consent of the majority of the people. It is now clear, for example, that in war-time Germany the Nazi government felt unable to impose on the German people the controls and the restraints which were imposed in Britain by the democratically elected government. Dictatorship may seem more efficient because in theory it gives government much more power, but in practice no government can make its will effective without a broad measure of consent, and where this consent is missing no amount of terror or secret police will produce the same response.

But although democracy is and will remain the ideal for Christians it is not part of basic Christian doctrine and even since the Reformation 'one man, one vote' has not been the rule for most of the time in many countries holding the Protestant faith. Nevertheless the Protestant countries adopted the principle of representative government early on and moved gradually towards universal suffrage and as the consequences of the Reformation worked themselves out 'one man, one vote' became increasingly common in Protestant countries. It is also interesting that it is only in Protestant countries that democracy has taken deep and lasting root. The countries with the longest history of democracy are Scandinavia, Holland, Switzerland, the United Kingdom, America, Canada, Australia and New Zealand, all of which are predominantly Protestant. Democracy in Japan is of very recent origin and almost entirely due to the influence of the United States since World War II. The democratic ideals of the Indian rulers came largely from the education of their first leaders in England. Democracy has had a chequered career in France, Italy and Greece and has been almost non-existent in Spain, Portugal and Eastern Europe. The only country which does not fit the pattern easily is Germany, which had a nominal Protestant majority but where the liberal movement failed to gain a lasting hold. But at the time when other Protestant countries were moving more firmly towards democracy, the leaders of German thought were already moving towards the philosophic paganism which was to be so catastrophic for the rest of Europe in the first half of the twentieth century. That Western Germany has now enjoyed twenty years of democracy is largely due to the influence of the major occupying powers, Britain and the United States, after the Second World War. The same can probably be said for Austria and Italy.

Since democracy requires the continued support of the whole country it can never be assured for all time. This must make it somewhat precarious in countries where there is a large Communist minority. It must be supported by the great majority of the country's non-political elite and, most important, by the civil service and the armed forces. Democratically elected politicians should command their respect, or at least the support for the system, even when there is no respect for the man. This is why civilian control of the armed forces is such a vital principle that any democrat must support it—even where the soldiers appear to be right and the politicians appear to be wrong.

But if trust and respect between the politician and the permanent establishment is necessary to democracy, trust between politicians is even more necessary. The difference between the 'social democracy' of the Communist powers and the democratic system evolved by countries in the Christian tradition is that the latter involves alternative governments and the former does not. The real test of a democracy is that a government in full control of the armed forces and the apparatus of

State voluntarily relinquishes its power to its opponents on its electoral defeat. There are some post-war democracies which have not yet had to face this critical test. This requires that politicians trust their opponents in office not to use their power unfairly to extend their term of office. Democracy also requires an electorate who will abide by the constitution when their party is voted out of office and who will not use direct action to retain their party in power. This in turn requires that the party in power is tolerant of those who oppose it and will not take measures which threaten their whole way of life.

Democracy also requires that politicians in power do not become arrogant and that even when they have a long period of office ahead or seem secure in power they are nevertheless sensitive to the feelings and views of the electorate as a whole. Of course government must govern and no self-respecting government should allow itself to be harried by temporary pressure into doing something which it knows to be wrong. Politicians are leaders and it is the job of the leader to lead. But part of the art of leadership is to try to obtain a consensus and to create the support that is necessary for the successful carrying out of policies. If this is not done, if leaders do not bother to muster public opinion behind them but go off wantonly on their own, despite the public consensus against them, they do great damage to the authority of the government. If, for this or any other reason, government creates disillusion and the disillusion persists for long enough, then there is usually a great upheaval in society which more often than not makes matters worse. In the early 1930s disillusion in America produced Roosevelt and the New Deal but disillusion in Germany produced Hitler and the Nazis.

Disillusion with democracy is not always the fault of government or of politicians. People often become disillusioned because of prior false illusions. Had they been more realistic, more level-headed, they would not have gone overboard for an idea or a man and they would not then react so violently when their hopes were dashed. Part of the illusion that new men or new policies will introduce the millennium arises from a false view of human ability which the well-instructed Christian should not share. A Washington or a Churchill can of course rouse men and make a whole nation rise above itself, but except in moments of national crisis, government is not usually conducted at this pitch and it would probably be unhealthy if it were.

The cynicism about politics and politicians which can be found in Christian circles has other causes. Many Christians find something rather distasteful about the artificial game of party politics and about the whole process of democratic elections. To many people there is something ludicrous and undignified about the whole political process. As Winston Churchill once said, democracy is a terrible way of choosing a government—except that every other known way is worse. People of principle particularly dislike having to stand on a broad political platform. They would prefer to stick to their own narrower range of personal principles. But in a democracy, government must obtain a consensus over a very wide front to support its actions and the two or three party system seems the best way so far devised to do this. With ten or twenty parties it would be far easier to obtain a consensus within a party, but it would then be very much more difficult to put together a government which could act at all effectively. In a two-party system, the party with a majority in the country has got enough public support to govern effectively. But the two-party system requires a coalition of interests within the party and a good part of the art of politics is the balancing of the interests and ideals of the different parts of the party. I cannot see that there is anything wrong in representing genuine interests within the body politic provided this is plainly and explicitly done. Nor can I see that there is anything wrong in the process of negotiating for your interests and ideals with others who have slightly different interests and ideals—conceding a point to gain a point and finally hammering out a national programme. Nor do I see anything wrong in explaining to your constituents the conditions under which their ideals and interests can be met.

Each man must decide for himself which of the great national parties is the coalition of interests and ideals best able to fulfil the ideals which he himself holds. No one will ever find a party which perfectly represents his own ideals. He has to recognise that it will also want to fulfil other ideals and that these may sometimes cross his own, but he will normally remain a loyal member so long as his own ideals remain in prospect and others do not cut across them too much.

While politics is about ideals, it is also based on the realities of power and a Christian should be a realist as well as an idealist. He should know the sources of political strength and the causes of political weakness. From my reading of history and my own brief experience I think that the main sources of political strength lie in the ability to resign, in the ability to carry conviction with those who have elected you and in the ability to persuade colleagues. The Christian should be free from the over-riding sense of ambition which makes it impossible for a man to resign; he should have the honesty and trustworthiness which enables him to carry conviction with his constituents and he should have the strength of will to work hard and to master his subject which will go a long way in helping him to carry his colleagues. If the Christian finally gets to a position of real power, then he, more than other men, should be capable of remembering that power must not be used wantonly or selfishly, but that it is held by him in trust for his fellow-men. Any fool can be a cynic and help to destroy trust in government by consent. It is therefore a special tragedy when Christians who should have the very qualities which make democracy work, content themselves with sneering with the cynics.

Democracy today is in danger from a number of other directions. Perhaps the most important of these, because the least obvious, is the appeal which the executive can now make directly to the people over the heads of their elected representatives. The logical extension of this is the use of the referendum, where the choice is made by the voter and not by the legislature. The danger is that the process of involving the elector directly appears to be more democratic. But the ordinary elector is no match for the executive. He needs his elected representatives to safeguard him and anything which cuts away their support will in the long run be damaging to the interests of the electorate. If the executive can win elections by direct appeal over television to the electorate and without the support of the individual elected representatives and if the latter are elected solely on a party ticket, then the position of the executive is not counter-balanced. Although in theory the opposition parties are a counter-balance to the executive they can only exercise this counter-balance in an election every four or five years. It seems to me that respect for the individual demands that he is not treated as a digit in a referendum but that he is able to elect someone whom he knows and trusts to a position sufficiently powerful to safeguard his interests against the acts of the executive government.

The ability of the elected representative to get known in his constituency and to gain himself the kind of reputation which can survive temporary opposition to his party leaders seems to me to demand some devolution of government from the centre. The more highly centralised a government is, the less can the individual's reputation count for anything and the more must we be dependent on the mass communication media and on the party ticket. That is part of the case for a partial devolution from a federal government to a provincial or state government. Most of the major democracies have this two-tier government; the major exception is the United Kingdom where perhaps because of its small geographical size, power has normally been centralised at Westminster. Even the United Kingdom, how-ever, is now examining the structure of its local government and is likely in the next few years to produce a more powerful second tier. One danger of a powerful provincial or state government is that it is more likely to have a built-in majority and its minority, deprived of the prospect of power, has to look to the federal government for protection. Britain's only pro-vincial government, the government of Northern Ireland, has had a Unionist majority and a Nationalist minority ever since 1923 when it was set up. The government of the United Kingdom regard it as their job to see that the Nationalists do not suffer because of their minority position. This guardian-ship of the constitution is a key function of federal government. Indeed, it was the last remaining function of the British Imperial government after the Dominions had become self-governing in every other way. For this reason states' rights, important though they are, ought never to be used to bolster the position of the majority against the minority. Indeed the use of states' rights for this purpose tends to damage the whole concept of the second tier of government and to concentrate power at the centre.

Another danger to democracy is the glamour attached to success, the stigma attached to the failure and the philosophy that 'politics is about power', the view that the 'winner takes all'. Of course the whole electoral apparatus is set up as a contest for office and in that sense politics is about power. But the more that politics is about power and power alone, the less is it likely to be about principles. The more a politician wants power and power alone, the less likely is he to stand firm about what he believes to be right, the more will he concentrate on putting up a show and the less will he pledge himself to doing anything in particular. The opinion polls help this trend along by concentrating everyone's mind in an election on predictions of the result rather than on the issues at stake. The question is no longer what the parties stand for but which of them will win.

The British and Canadian parliamentary system which gives a constitutional standing to the leader of the opposition seems preferable to the American system where the defeated Presidential candidate loses everything, including a base from which he can run again. The parliamentary system enabled Winston Churchill, excluded from office in 1931, to continue to fight in Parliament for rearmament and a tough foreign policy towards the European dictatorships. It enabled him to gather round him the political support and eventually the national support which brought him to office as Prime Minister in 1940. Government is not just a game with winners and losers, it is far more important. It is about ideals and the means of realising those ideals and for the Christian it must be better to lose with honour than to win by throwing over the causes for which he stands.

Of course ideals cannot be so rigid that we lose all flexibility in government and of course they must be tempered to meet the world as it is. To some people ideals become a rigid ideology which is a substitute for thought and of course politics demands compromise if government is to be effective, but there comes a point where the man who is interested in power alone will be prepared to make one compromise too many, but where the man of principle will decide that 'enough is enough'.

The ultimate danger to democracy, however, comes from ideologies which do not respect the individual as a responsible being answerable to God for all that he does. Atheistic Communism is prepared to subordinate the individual to the good of the community, but outside those democracies with a large Communist party, such as Italy and France, the danger to democracy today does not come from Communism but from humanism. At the entrance of the Czech pavilion in Expo 67 stood a plaque which said something to the effect that Communism (they may have called it Socialism) was the heritage of the humanism of all the ages. There is a stronger connection between Communism and humanism than most Western humanists will admit, but in the West humanism has inherited much of the Christian's care for the individual and Christianity's conscience about the individual's suffering and his needs. The danger would come if the influence of Christianity were to grow less and the logic of humanism were to be followed more thoroughly to its conclusions. Western scientific humanism has not yet been able to decide between the two conflicting objectives of the complete freedom of the individual (a freedom Christians might regard as licence) and the fullest and most rapid application of technological advance. The logic of Communism has led them to choose the latter. The success of democratic economies has so far enabled most Western countries to avoid a choice. But if the democratic economies slow down and falter, the pressure will be on. Too often in Britain I have heard the question, 'What will you do if the voluntary method fails?'

Another danger of a thorough going secular society based on humanist philosophy lies in its failure to recognise the nature of evil and in its need to substitute the general good of the community for the absolute law of God. Despite the unparalleled forces of evil unleashed in the twentieth century, humanists still regard evil as something which is susceptible to corrective treatment if only they can discover what that treatment is. Consequently, their attitude to crime leans heavily towards the correction of the criminal as someone not wholly well in his mind. They dislike the idea of punishment of the criminal as a responsible individual who has offended not just the laws of man but the law of God. These attitudes can only detract from the dignity and responsibility of man but, more dangerous still, if the laws of men are to be based on the convenience of society and not on the law of God, then there is nothing to stop the extension of law to cover any action which the majority in society temporarily regard as offensive. Laws based on the convenience of the temporary majority in society can soon become oppressive to the liberties of the minority. Humanism is, however, unlikely to displace democracy unaided. It is an intellectual system with little appeal to the average man. The much greater danger is that it will undermine the principles on which democratic rule is based and make it liable to collapse in the face of an autocratic bid for power.

Another possible danger to democracy is that it may become discredited by its introduction in countries which previously have only known paternalistic rule. Personally, I believe that even if this is a risk, it is one worth taking. In any case, the main period of transition to self-government from imperial rule — or from the rule of an occupying power — is now over and while not all the newly constituted governments have survived in democratic form, the original democratic constitution may well be an ideal to which they can at some point return. I was once in a small group at a reception where a Communist Ambassador was questioning a guest who had been the British High Commissioner in a newly independent territory. The Ambassador was asking in a puzzled way why Britain insisted on translating the whole democratic apparatus of Westminster into the middle of Africa. The ex-High Commissioner replied simply that that was what the Africans wanted. They felt that their dignity as human beings required 'one man, one vote' and for this purpose they regarded the Westminster model as the best they knew. In fact, in the territory to which that High

Commissioner had been accredited, parliamentary democracy has so far survived, as it has in all the countries occupied by the Western democracies after World War II.

But although the Christian may regard democracy as being the ideal form of government, he should recognise that its success does depend on the kind of conditions we have outlined and that failing these conditions, it would almost certainly be displaced by one-party rule, by military dictatorship, or by some kind of feudal oligarchy. If the democrat continues to press for democratic rule, as the United States has done in South Vietnam, it is because people are more likely to behave responsibly when they are given responsibility. Furthermore, an outsider given a temporary say in another nation's affairs must do his best to hand back control to the people as a whole, whatever they may subsequently do with the control that he has given them. It would, for instance, have been intolerable had Germany, Austria, Italy and Japan not been given democratic governments after World War II but had instead been handed over to an autocracy on the basis that they were not yet fit for democratic rule.

If nations with a Christian ethic are to propagate the idea of the dignity and responsibility of the individual then they must do it whole-heartedly. Indeed, one of the dangers which Western democracies face is that in making too sharp a division between the Communist and non-Communist world they are in danger of seeming to forget that the menace to individual dignity and freedom can be just as great in non-Communist as in Communist countries. While it may be perfectly correct to see a non-Communist dictator as a useful military ally and to worry about the military consequences of a Communist take-over in his country, the democratic countries should, if they want their ideals to be believed, take care to distinguish between friendships of ideology and friendships of convenience. Communism may end up as an oppressive oligarchy but this is not apparent to the Asian peasant to whom it offers liberation from an already oppressive feudal landlord, and it will be better for the democracies in the battle of ideas if they do not always seem to be on the side of the landlords.

(ii) RELATIONS BETWEEN NATIONS

The Christian should not only think out his ideals for the political system of his own country but should also have some guide posts to his country's attitude to other nations. It is a commonplace among politicians that, except in time of war, voters are not much interested in external affairs. State departments, foreign offices and chancellories do not come under much political pressure from their own electorates and yet the great democracies exercise a tremendous influence in the world and their actions and policies are vital to the peace and welfare of most other countries. It creates the worst possible impression in the rest of the world if the electorates in the democracies seem to care only about the domestic actions of their own governments, the actions which affect them personally, and to care very much less about the effect of their governments' actions abroad. The more powerful and wealthy a country is, the more vital are its external actions.

Diplomacy is mainly concerned with trade and defence and in both of these a country will need partners. War produces some very odd partners, countries thrown together with nothing in common but the common enemy. Even military treaties and defence arrangements can be drawn up not because countries have a common ideology but as the lesser of two evils. But permanent trading arrangements, by which countries voluntarily become interdependent in order to improve their prosperity and strengthen their economies, are best made between countries with a strong mutual affinity. The Latin-American Free Trade Area, the Nordic Customs Union, the Benelux Customs Union, the European Economic Community, and the European Free Trade Association are all associations where most of the partners have an identity of outlook. Competition from partners in a trading area produces strains on the partnership. The lowering of tariff barriers sets up new forces of competition which threaten old-established industries and the trading area treaties take out of the hands of sovereign governments remedies which they used to have to protect the employment of their people. When these pressures arise, a strong tide of goodwill towards the country's trading partners and towards the ideal of greater prosperity through freer trade is necessary to counter the domestic protectionist lobbies. But it is well worth all the fuss and bother because the creation of these international partnerships and the breaking down of international suspicion and hostility can do an enormous amount towards improving the real wealth of the world. I believe that any Christian should throw himself wholeheartedly into the creative work of forging these international links.

Everyone is, of course, entitled to try to strike the best bargain for the country he represents, but what matters is not the tough bargaining session but the will to make a bargain. The bargaining atmosphere is as important at the business level as at the diplomatic. The Christian engaged in international business can do a great deal to help international understanding by his fairness in striking a bargain and sticking to it, by his persistence in trying to find solutions to difficult problems and by providing safeguards and assurances to overcome the real risks of international trade. The international business man can do an enormous amount of hurt or harm his country's image and to promote understanding between nations. Nothing, in fact, is more fascinating than international business and nothing gives a greater insight into national character than haggling over a tough business bargain. When the Italian tariffs were coming down to the common external level of the European Economic Community, the American companies were able for the first time to compete on roughly level terms in Italy with the big Italian companies. I remember trying to reconcile the divergent business philosophies of an Italian and an American tycoon. The Italian was outraged that the American was undercutting the Italian published price in offers to the Italian's long-established customers. This offended his concepts of orderly marketing and the maintenance of established connections. The American was equally outraged that the Italian was giving secret over-riding discounts below his published price. This offended his concepts of open dealing. I didn't think I had got much further in international conciliation than making both of

7

them see that the other had a legitimate point, but soon after I heard that the Italian had taken the lesson to heart and was over in America using the American pricing policies and getting a bit of his own back.

Just as important as international trade, is international investment, and banking. The free movement of capital is a tremendous aid to world trade. Yet anyone who has had large amounts of money invested in someone else's country will know the anxieties and tensions to which this gives rise on both sides. The local labour force are aware that the ultimate control of their destinies is in some distant city and is exercised by men whose way of life they do not understand and whom they may, to a greater or less extent, distrust. The local government suspect that the pricing system milks off the profits earned in their country, that the products from their country are kept out of markets reserved for the parent company's products. However, the international business community has, by and large, adopted ethical standards which make overseas enterprise acceptable and profitable to the host country, the investor and the employee. It is perhaps worth noticing in passing that most international investment comes from the old democracies.

International banking does not have quite the same reputation for helping the countries on the receiving end. This is, I imagine, because an industrial investment once made is more or less irreversible. The company cannot suddenly decide to remove a plant which it has put down overseas. Once the money has been sunk, it is irreversibly committed. A flow of hot money, on the other hand, can be reversed overnight to the great damage of the country which loses it. The international bankers who call their money back in a hurry and for no apparent reason are still mistrusted and feared. In Britain, which has had more than its fair share of movements of 'hot money' they are now commonly known as the 'gnomes of Zürich'. This is certainly unfair to Zürich and to the international banking community, who are bound to conduct their business on the rules as they find them. But the folklore does show the need for a great deal more co-operation in international monetary arrangements than governments have so far achieved.

Second only to war, the greatest threat to international prosperity is almost certainly the mistrust by countries of each other's currency and the continued dependence on gold as the final means of settlement of international accounts. Almost all the burden of running international currencies now falls upon Britain and America and for Britain the burdens are beginning to outweigh the benefits. It is absurd that currencies should still have to have as their backing a commodity of very limited practical use, mined at enormous expense and producing no revenue when, if men could only trust each other more, currencies could be backed by the real revenue-earning resources of the nations which issue them. It is a real tragedy that the wealth of nations cannot develop as fast as it might because countries cannot be induced to make the necessary additions to the holding of each other's currencies. If nations had the same mistrust of their own currency, if everyone kept his savings in the mattress and there had been no bank liquidity to help expand the nation's business, we should all still be intolerably poor and for no good reason. International liquidity is one of the great remaining areas for further international co-operation. The Christian virtues of trustworthiness and care for the needs and sensibilities of others are vital to international investment and international banking and finance. It is hard to say how much world trade depends on the Christian ethic, but I would suspect that the dependence is much greater than most people realise. It is interesting that international banking is heavily based on those countries which have traditionally accepted the Christian ethic.

Although the Christian must be concerned in his country's support for world peace and for the improvement of world trade, he should also take an intense interest in the practice of religious toleration. We are at present in a rather odd phase in which some Western patterns of life—such as the primacy of economic objectives—have temporarily confused the Eastern religions and have thoroughly disrupted tribal society. No strong ideology meantime, except in Communist countries, has taken the place of the old religions and the secular rulers of most non-Communist countries are still uneasily neutral towards religion. Some Catholic and some Mohammedan countries are an exception to this. But the short war between India and Pakistan, between Hindu and Muslim, and the animosity between Mohammedan and Jew in the near East show that whatever the constitutions of modern States, intolerant ideology is not far below the surface. On the other hand, the gradual opening up of eastern Europe and Russia has probably made Communist ideology less rigid. The best course for the Christian and for the country trying to base its policy on Christian principles is to keep up continuous diplomatic pressure for religious liberty. One particularly intolerant country recently made substantial moves towards religious liberty solely because of the acute embarrassment caused to it by its intolerant reputation. I have more than once introduced the subject of religious toleration in conversation with Communist diplomats and ministers. It may have done no good, but I am almost certain that it cannot have done any harm and in the long run continued pressure like this is bound to have some effect. We have to remember that when Communists think of Christianity, they are thinking not of the Protestant Churches, but of other Churches whose record of religious toleration and involvement in politics made them formidable opponents.

In international affairs we should distinguish those we temporarily want to influence from those who are our genuine and lasting friends. The trouble with friends is that they often speak their minds much more openly and brusquely to each other than they do to those whom they either fear or distrust. In the English-speaking world in particular we are all far more rude to each other than to those who do not have the common language. We operate a kind of double standard. We are quite prepared to criticise each other on race relations when we would never dream of criticising a Mohammedan for his attitude to women or a Hindu for his attitude to caste. We shout our heads off about civil rights in America and are quite prepared to ignore the almost complete lack of civil rights in dozens of other nations. Up to a point this is justified on the grounds that in the English-speaking world we can expect to have some influence on each other and therefore it is worth making a fuss, whereas elsewhere we are unlikely to achieve much for our effort. But if we are not to find ourselves friendless in a hard world we ought every now and again to recognise the nations with whom we have so much in common and whom, in a tough spot, we would really trust to come to our help.

But above all, a Christian attitude to international affairs should be balanced and should avoid violent emotional swings. We should be realistic about philosophies which are alien to our own Christian faith and to the way of life based on a Christian culture. But this is no excuse for the wild hates and witch-hunts which from time to time can sweep across a nation. While loyalty to one's country is a strong and necessary cohesive force, it is also a force that can run wild and do untold damage.

Many Christians feel that there is something wrong about the exercise of power politics, especially in the domination of the world by great powers. The ideal of today is the United Nations with its General Assembly where each power, however small, has a vote. Yet why should a tiny power with less than a million people rank equally to the United States or the U.S.S.R. with two hundred millions? On the other hand, if voting were by population and China were admitted, with over six hundred million people it would dominate the Assembly. There seems to be no easy solution. It is arguable that, in practice, the United Nations can only operate in peripheral areas where great power interests are not involved. The U.N. could do nothing about the Hungarian Revolution of 1956 or the Cuban missile crisis. Indeed, the very constitution of the U.N. with its Security Council of great powers, each of which has a veto, shows that the great powers have explicitly said that they will not let it interfere with their vital interests, their spheres of influence. These spheres of influence protect the peace within the sphere and the balance of power between nations. Nations have tried to keep a balance of power to prevent the danger and corruption to society when one power has a potentially tyrannical dominance. In Europe before the Second World War the balance of power was not upset by the German annexation of Austria. It even survived the military extinction of Czecho- slovakia — though one wonders whether the Czechs would have yielded so quickly to the Communist *coup d'état* in 1948 had the great democracies come to their aid ten years earlier. But when Hitler took Czechoslovakia, Britain and France both gave notice, by signing a defence treaty with Poland, that they considered that the German annexation of Poland would tilt the European balance of power too heavily in favour of Germany and that they would resist it.

Those who oppose the concept of the balance of power between spheres of influence of great States must answer for the results to the world were America once more to become isolationist. Western Europe, weakened after the Second World War, swung into the American sphere of influence. American protection was extended from the North Cape to Eastern Turkey and for this every European has cause to be grateful. What European can deny to Japan and south-east Asia the protection which they once enjoyed? What American can justify the withdrawal of protection when it can be afforded and when so many countries in the free world depend on it? The slowness of Britain's disengagement from the far East and the reluctance with which her allies let her go, show that the sphere of influence can have a real and useful function.

It is important however that we should not confuse the maintenance of international equipoise through balance of power with ideological conflict. It so happens that the Christian position is opposed to atheistic Communism. But the Christian position is equally opposed to other religions and ideologies and a nation purporting to hold Christian principles has no justification for embarking on a military crusade against those holding other views. It is our business to convert and to win those with other views and not to kill them. We have to remember that we were very glad of the help of Communist Russia in defeating Nazi Germany and Fascist Italy. Indeed, in sheer numbers of men lost they bore the brunt of the struggle. If we base our international line-up on ideology and not on the balance of power then we cannot but look hypocrites when we call in aid the arms of Fascist States or corrupt oligarchies who happen to be within our sphere of influence. Ideological struggle, apart from being wrong in principle, makes us go through ridiculous contortions to appear to agree with those who happen, as the lesser of two evils, to be necessary allies. And finally by making the struggle ideological we help to close the minds of all those in the other spheres of influence to the Christian message which they will identify as the ideology of their enemies. The Christian message is universal and must not appear to be the prerogative of one group of powers.

Of course spheres of influence are not entirely dependent on physical power and we ought not to minimise the part played by ideology. Stalin at the height of his power was advised not to take a certain action because it might offend the Pope. Contemptuously he asked 'and how many divisions has the Pope?' But the question only displayed his ignorance of foreign affairs because, in a sense, the armies of every Catholic country were the Pope's divisions. Yet the refusal of the West to go to the aid of Hungary in 1956 and the dismantling of the Cuban missile sites in 1962 showed that, in a crisis, the recognition of a great power sphere of influence was more important than ideology. The influence and power of a great nation is one of the facts of life in a world made mistrustful by sin and even a nation most fully alive to Christian ideals has to live with this fact as best it may. Indeed, one of the dilemmas facing Britain today is that although it is heavily over-stretched in maintaining its old sphere of influence from the Persian Gulf to Singapore and although it holds no worthwhile territory in the whole of this great area, simply a residual string of bases, nevertheless it has hesitated overtly to abandon the area lest other ambitious powers are tempted to claim the inheritance and the peace of the world is disturbed in the scramble to take over. Every economic argument on withdrawal was countered by the question, 'but what would happen if we went?' There would be a great power vacuum which more than one power would want to fill and, according to this argument, the resultant release of pressure would be bound to produce conflict. (At the time of writing the decision has been made to come out by 1972, but the Opposition seem pledged to stay and a general election is due not later than 1971.)

Britain may have felt bound to impose sanctions on Rhodesia

because of its obligation to the disfranchised majority. But quite apart from this, Britain could not renounce its sovereignty over this small nation without opening up central Africa to the outside intervention of another great power, to anyone who might have been called in to help an African nation suffering defeat in armed conflict.

Those of us in Britain who felt that our island economy would not stand our present overstretched international commitments, had a tough job in persuading even those in whom we might expect the anti-imperialist feelings to be strongest. At a diplomatic reception, I was in a group with a Kenyan, an Iranian and an American and asked them all whether they agreed that Britain ought to cut its commitments east of Suez and withdraw its forces from the area. All of them were utterly opposed to the idea and all felt that the British military presence provided security and stability. For a sphere of influence is not just a device to keep the balance between great powers. Its other function is to keep peace and stability between minor powers and to keep the trade routes free.

The most acute difficulties come at the junctions of the great powers' spheres of influence. Once a great power suffers defeat on the boundary, its whole sphere of protection and of influence is called in question. Russia fought in Hungary because it feared for the stability of Communist regimes in Eastern Europe. Kennedy feared what Russian intervention in Cuba would do in Latin America. In the late sixties the most critical intervention has been in Vietnam where neither great power felt able to abandon its client state.

It is a legitimate function of a great power to help to maintain world order because there will be disorder and confusion if it does not. The world is not naturally an orderly place and the extent to which smaller powers can maintain order around them is limited. We take it for granted today that there is no piracy on the high seas. But piracy did not disappear by magic. It disappeared because the warships of great powers patrolled the oceans. Even this century has known arbitrary war-lords capable of exercising petty sovereignty over large areas and of exacting tribute from all who pass through their territories. At one time, Mao Tse-tung was one of the Chinese war-lords. The withdrawal of the Belgians from the Congo shows what chaos can result from a great power vacuum and how easily the peace, security and stability which we take so much for granted depends on the background sanction of military power. Most empires of the past have grown, not because anyone wanted them to grow, but because there was always trouble at the periphery which in the end was usually settled by the subjugation of yet another province. But if a great power can legitimately help to maintain order in the world it must respect other great powers which are fulfilling the same function.

It is therefore quite wrong to treat the exercise of a great power's influence within its sphere in the same way as a major war between great powers. America, with the backing of the Western world was perfectly correct to resist the North Korean invasion of South Korea but I believe that President Truman was equally correct to refuse his army commanders permission to enter the territory of mainland China, because this took the war outside America's sphere of influence. As it was, the Chinese felt bound to intervene when the U.S. military commanders overran the Chinese client state.

But perhaps the greatest lesson of recent times is that a great power must remember always to act in the interests of the inhabitants of the area where it exercises influence. An operation in any other country's territory, even within a sphere of influence, must be conducted for the benefit of the inhabitants of that territory and if it ceases to be of benefit to them, the operation ceases to have any virtue. Although the realities of international power may be harsh, the style in which that power is exercised must never appear to be harsh. The British took six or seven years to free Malaya of guerillas. This could only be done by the gradual and patient clearing of area after area. As the local population came to realise by experience that the forces of the Malayan government were in fact in control and were there in their interests and for their security, they ceased to fear the guerillas and came to trust the government. After seven years of painstaking effort, of securing village after village,

the whole territory was ultimately made secure. The same
tactics were employed with Mau Mau in Kenya and with the
infiltration in North Borneo and Sarawak in the last three
years. To have treated these as purely military operations, run
on military lines, would have been to alienate the population
whose security and prosperity the great power was there to
provide. As the Nazis found in occupied Europe, brutality does
not pay. A great power is only justified in having a sphere of
influence if it is wanted by the nations in that sphere. If its behaviour makes it first resented and then hated, it will have to
pour in more and more force in order to hold down less and less
territory and in the end, despite the added power which
industrial society gives to the strong nation, it will be bound to
fail. A sphere of influence is not the same as a sphere of military
control.

It also follows that if a great power is to provide for the
prosperity of its sphere of influence it should provide both aid
and investment to the less powerful countries in the area. But
here too the manner and style of the aid and help is important.
Those providing aid are not in charge of an endless cornucopia
and they owe it both to their own people, who have to provide
the money through taxes, and to those who live in the countries
being helped, to see that the funds which are allocated do the
greatest possible good. There is, for instance, the very real
problem of corruption if funds are not channelled through a
reputable and well-policed organisation. There is also the problem of seeing that aid funds go to meet the real needs of a
country rather than unrealisable ambitions of national self-
sufficiency or useless prestige projects. It is a perfectly legitimate
objective for a country to want to diversify from the production
of a basic commodity such as cocoa, rice or copper on which it
is far too heavily dependent; but there is not much point in
erecting a prestige steel works which requires a lot of capital and
employs comparatively few people. It would seem far more
sensible to start consumer industries which employ more people
and need less capital.

A steady flow of private investment is also essential to the
well-being of the less developed countries. The host country

may have its anxieties but the investor in a less-developed country can face many hazards too, penal taxation, blocked currency, legal penalties against any reduction in numbers employed and finally, expropriation without adequate compensation. I think that in my time in international business I have faced all these and other hazards. On the other hand there are the benefits of tax holidays, less competition and lower wage costs. However, the greatest hazard at present to private overseas investment is the lack of international liquidity and the pressure on sterling and the dollar, which puts pressure on both Britain and America to reduce their capital outlay. Although both countries try to safeguard the flow of capital to the less-developed countries, it is almost impossible for governments to police the flow of funds and a lack of liquidity is almost certain to hit the developing countries hardest.

More important than aid and more important than private investment are the less-developed countries' access to the great industrial markets of the world and the continued growth of those markets. The industrial nations are the pace-setters of economic growth. The price of basic commodities depends heavily on the volume of world trade and for this reason, if for no other, the industrial countries should make every effort to maintain a reasonable rate of economic growth. Aid can never fill the gap caused by a decline in a country's revenue-earning capacity. And because access to industrial markets is so vital, the industrialised countries should not, in their trading arrangements, fail to give a progressively improving position to the less developed countries.

The other great problem facing the industrialised countries is the immigration from less-developed countries. Canada and the United States have made a tremendous success of immigration, though for Britain this is a relatively new problem. But modern communications and the great difference in incomes between countries will make for hard decisions in immigration policy in all the industrial nations. Any country which invited a completely open entry would be asking for the destruction of any cohesion in its society, so that however strong a country's Christian principles it should still exercise a control over immigration. Not only should a country be able to house, educate and give medical care to immigrants but immigration should not exceed the rate of social assimilation. It is no part of racial tolerance to pretend that all races have the same habits and culture and it is only realistic to assume that new-comers will take time to adapt to the culture and way of life of their new-found country. If they come in at too fast a rate there will inevitably be pressure to seal them off and this will have the effect of perpetuating divisions. On the other hand, those who do come should expect to be treated as equals in a society with the same rights and privileges. For the Christian there is 'neither Jew nor Gentile, bond or free'. All the English-speaking countries, Britain included, have been enormously strengthened by immigrants.

There is, however, another side to the coin. What one country gains from immigrants another country loses. Britain and North America have had their fair share of refugees from oppression elsewhere. Britain had first the Jews, then the Huguenots and in the eighteenth and nineteenth centuries there was a great tide westward from feudal and backward countries. What those countries lost was probably their own fault. But it is quite another thing to go out and use your greater resources to cream the expensively educated skilled manpower from other free and democratic countries leaving them with an ever increasing proportion of unskilled and elderly. It may seem legitimate to a country to bid in the world market for talent on the grounds that its ability to pay more for talent shows that it is capable of making better use of the talent it gets than those who cannot match its offers. But if this were carried to its logical conclusion it would condemn less-advanced countries to perpetual backwardness or force them in desperation to build physical barriers like the Berlin wall. If a country is to be fair it should allow entry to a complete cross-section of young and old, skilled and unskilled, otherwise it would seem only right to make some compensation to the country which is being drained of the skills which its educational system has produced.

Although not strictly within the subject of the relations

between nations, it is hardly possible to pass by the subject of Christian missions, for it is on this personal level that understanding is built and that the Christian message makes its most immediate and most permanent impact. Our Lord has told us to go out into all the world and preach the gospel to every nation. In the last two centuries the Christian Church has done just that. Almost every Church in Britain, Canada and the United States will have a missionary for whom it prays, to whom it writes and from whom it hears. It will know far more than the embassy officials about the real quality of life in the up-country villages, the poverty and disease, the habits and prejudices of the villagers. It will know some of their names and will pray for them by name. It will know of those who profess conversion, those who fall away, those who return again. It will understand, as no government official can understand, the power of the witch-doctor, of voodoo, of ju-ju. Every four or five years, the church's missionary will return and will tell the story of his work with colour slides and film and the Church will go over the Andes, up the Amazon, into the jungle of Borneo and over the Himalaya. No one who does not understand the involvement of the Church in mission work can ever understand the shock in Britain and in North America of the Communist take-over in China. This was not some remote country of the inscrutable East, but the land of Pastor Hsi, whose cities, rivers, mission stations and churches were the familiar background on ten thousand church halls. It was not the land of the geographic magazine, but of the Boxer rising, the martyrdom of John and Betty Stam, of Gladys Aylward's trek through no-man's-land with her orphans. Yet through all this, the Christian gospel was preached, men and women were converted and the lives of whole communities were transformed; until 1948, when every white man was expelled, however long he had lived there, however much he had helped, and the connection with the outside world brought to an abrupt and complete end. Familiar landmarks, familiar friends, the object of prayer, of thought, of gifts, of a lifetime's service of sons, daughters, brothers and sisters had been brought to an abrupt and apparently untimely end.

Yet the lessons of China have been learned and today the Churches of Africa, of Asia, of South America are perhaps less dominated by the foreign missionary and foreign culture, less dependent on foreign aid, and more capable of standing on their own feet. Missionaries are more aware of the need to make sure that they are preaching the Christian faith and not the Western way of life, more aware of the need to care, as Our Lord did, for the body as well as for the soul, and today find themselves not only delivering, but also receiving the impact of the 'culture shock'.

But there are still lessons to be learned. Churches at home would serve the missionfield best if they did not put so much emphasis on visible results. 'One soweth and another reapeth.' The sowing may take years and the sower should not be forced to produce artificial results to get the support he needs to stay in the field. Churches would also help if they did not insist on knowing better than the directors of the mission which individuals require support. It is desirable to keep a personal link, but those who are young, glamorous and personable, who have toured the home Churches telling of the work are not the only ones who need food, clothes, books, medicine and shelter.

On the missionfield itself, there always seems to be a need for more sympathy and understanding of an alien way of life. The more generously endowed the mission, the greater the danger that the compound will be cut off from life around, that material possessions will put a difference between two groups of Christians, will mark the missionary off more distinctly as a foreigner. Yet, so far as the Western culture genuinely derives from Christian values, the missionary must, in the end stand by what he believes. It is part of Christian instruction that we should redeem the time and not waste it. This is a discipline which is lacking in large parts of the world. The missionary must be patient when appointments are not kept, when people come in at any time and stay until any hour, but he must discipline himself. The belief that truth is right and falsehood wrong seems more deeply ingrained in countries with a Christian background. The missionary has to learn to put up with every different shade of grey, without himself departing from the truth. But all idea of racial or national superiority is to be avoided like the plague. All of his background which is merely the reflection of his own nation's habit, taste, temperament and fashion, is to be subservient to the needs of his work, to the bond of understanding he is trying to forge.

In an increasingly cosmopolitan world, those who stay at home are beginning to have the same opportunities and problems as the missionary. Universities in Britain and North America are full of overseas students, who will judge the Christian faith on the performance of those they meet who profess it. Those who will decide in ten and twenty years' time whether Christians should be free to worship and to propagate their faith in Africa and Asia are at present doing courses in Boston, in Montreal, in London. If they are not asked out to Christian homes, if they are treated as second-class citizens, if Christians seem smug and arrogant, then the Christian Church in their own country will have lost a friend and made an enemy. I sometimes wonder what would have happened to the course of history if some Christian had befriended Ho Chi Minh when he was a dish-washer in the Carlton Hotel in Pall Mall. On the other hand an African was once heard to say, after going round London trying to find a flat with his fiancée, 'It is only the Christians who care for us.'

To return to our main theme and to sum up, a democratic government can only pursue a really generous foreign policy if its citizens are as conscious of the needs of others as they are of their own. The Christian's interest in public affairs should not be confined to his own country or to missionary affairs in foreign countries. He should be interested in all the problems we have discussed, the growth of world trade, the value of the currency issued in his country's name, religious toleration, the maintenance of the peace, the provision of aid and trading opportunities to developing countries and, in reverse, the barriers his country imposes against the flow of trade and immigration laws which are fair to the nations losing skilled men and to those who want to come in.

But at this point of time, perhaps the greatest need is that those nations which have the same traditional ideals, which stand for the freedom of the individual, the rule of law, the development of economic opportunities for all, the dignity of labour, the emancipation of women, racial equality and religious tolerance; which are not only prepared to assent to these as platitudes, but put them into practice in their laws, constitutions, aid and trading policies; that these nations should support and strengthen each other to the maximum extent. Not only in defence, but also in trade and in international finance, power comes from unity. It is tempting for a nation to go its way; it requires less discipline, less patience, less understanding. It feels better not to be dependent on others, to ask no favours, to give the same treatment to all comers; but action requires that we have friends and that we have a framework of mutual obligation to make that friendship effective in action. The British Commonwealth has pioneered the way, but Britain now has too little of the benefits to carry the burdens unaided. What the world today requires from those nations with common ideals and the economic means, unitedly, to implement those ideals, is that they should join together and use their common strength to haul the poorer nations over the threshold of subsistence and into self-sustaining growth. It could be done and it is a cause worthy of the working lives of dedicated men and women.

(iii) INDUSTRIAL ETHICS

The power of government, great though it is, is limited in industrial society by the performance of the country's industrial machine. If this does well then government can have the money it needs for its social programmes and if there is enough money to go round and real incomes are steadily going forward then the edge and bitterness can be taken off social strife. Money may not buy everything but it is a tremendous help. What society needs from the industrial machine, which is the source of its income, is efficient performance. A great deal in the way of rough edges can be forgiven if the machine is producing the goods that society wants, in ever increasing volume. However, there is a division of interest between society in general and those who happen to be working in a particular corporation. The work force, of course, want performance too because their rate of pay in a particular job depends on the efficiency of the company they work for. But coupled with this they also want fair treatment, good management and good union representation. Each company has to balance its policies between performance and fair treatment of the work force. These are the issues which are hammered out between the union leaders arguing the case for fair treatment and the company officials arguing the case for economic performance. Ideally the management should obtain the kind of annual improvement in performance which would satisfy the legitimate needs of the work force without difficulty or conflict. Ideally the work force should be satisfied that the management were not cruising but were really working to produce the best possible performance from the company. Ideally the unions would realise their own responsibility for higher production and would not use the rules about their jobs to prevent the efficient operation of the plant. They would not try to extract the last penny in negotiation for every change in working methods. Ideally both management and unions would solve their problems by better performance and not by unloading the costs of the benefits demanded by the union on to the customer in higher prices or lower specification.

It is the ability, within limits, to fix its income by determining its price which distinguishes the industrial company from so many other organisations of society. Government, the teaching professions, the army, the law, the police, medicine, the Church, all represent enormous organisations in society but none of them is primarily an economic organisation. Many of them are protected by charter or law and governed by specific codes of ethics, but very few are entrepreneurial, promoting a demand for a product which otherwise might not be made or bought. It is this ability to create wealth, and, within limits, to allocate the wealth created, which gives business its unique independence. So long as it is profitable and can find new markets there is no formal limit to its expansion. A hospital is there to cure illness, not to create a demand for its services. Therefore there is some limit to a hospital's revenue. Most societies try to price

8

medical services so that they are within the reach of any section of society. But the company making a refrigerator is free to price it so that it obtains the maximum revenue over the useful life of the product.

The other source of autonomy in business is its very complexity. No government, speaking for society, is ever in a position to make the business-man's decision for him. A government may have to make military decisions, it may have to collect revenue, to administer the law and there is a sense in which all these things are complex. But there is a sense also in which government can understand what it is doing. Even when government has gone into a business on its own, when it is the owner of a large nationalised industry as so many European governments are, it is still very much in the hands of those who run the industry. When a nationalised industry wants to put its price up, government may delay the decision for a time but it finds it hard to dispute the industry's expert judgment. This inability of government to take responsibility for industrial decisions depends partly on the relative newness of large-scale industry. All the other matters about which government is concerned have been with it for a long time but complex and large-scale industry has only been with us for part of this century and it has grown in complexity and scale every year, so that by the time the outsider had written the textbook, he would probably be out of date.

Society does not usually like great forces over which it has no control and there is therefore likely to be continuing pressure for control over the industrial machine in some way or other. In the United States this has taken the form of the most elaborate and stringent anti-trust laws which, to the outsider, seem somewhat oppressive. In the smaller countries of Europe there is normally a close but informal relationship between government and the major industrial companies. In Continental Europe government exercises some control through the banking system, on which, because it does not have the highly developed capital markets of the Anglo-Saxon countries, industry is heavily dependent. In France, the degree of government control is probably at its highest since most companies carry a very heavy load of debt in relation to risk capital and are also subject to stiff price controls. My own belief is that since government can never fully understand the complex industrial machine, its attempts at direct control run the risk of being arbitrary and harmful and that business should set such high standards for itself and should enforce its standards so well that society does not make the mistake of trying to impose upon it the hamper of government control. The practical way of doing this would be to extend to business the kind of professional standards exercised by the older skills.

A profession of business management would not only set standards of fair treatment to employees, standards of disclosure to shareholders and other standards of high administration but should also attempt to set standards and ideals of economic performance. In other words no manager would be thought professionally competent who made continuous losses, even if he treated his employees well and disclosed his losses in full detail! If it is performance which society requires from business then the profession must set standards of performance.

Some of the very largest companies accounting for millions of pounds of shareholders' money and hundreds of thousands of employees should perhaps have some special responsibilities over and above those normally required by company law. Both in Britain and America the pattern of anti-trust has tended to allow the building up of enormous companies, yet it has prevented joint marketing arrangements, which would enable companies to retain the independence of their manufacturing unit, employing the bulk of their work force. It has forced them to merge completely or not at all. We should legislate to enable a company to obtain the market share it needed for economic survival, by merging its marketing arrangements alone and retaining independent control over its production.

We should recognise that labour unions perform a necessary function for employees, but we should see that there is a stronger relationship between a national union and the officials bargaining for the employees of a particular plant. The function of the national union is to see that those in a strong bargaining position do not get all the benefits at the expense of those whose bargaining position is temporarily weak. They must also see that the lower paid worker gets his fair share and that there is not too high a differential for those who have scarce skills. But just as government finds that the decisions of particular companies are so complex that only those who run the companies can sensibly make them, so a national union must ideally allow a great degree of autonomy to those representing the work force at plant level so that they can bargain with particular managements about particular conditions. Union officials should be given the money to do a proper job, including the job of communication between union headquarters and local branch. Union leaders should not press their temporary bargaining strength to the limit and employers should not take full advantage of their temporary bargaining weakness. Each side should remember that they have to live to fight another day.

The customer can operate the market forces against a company by shopping elsewhere but it is not right that the worker's only redress should be to go and work elsewhere. A worker requires collective bargaining to give some weight to his case. Finding another job may be a practical remedy for an individual in good times but if it were the only remedy it would cause oppression and hardship. The unions protect the liberty of the individual in a practical and workable way. Unions are weaker than corporations and we should almost certainly want to maintain legitimate union power. It is worth noticing that it is countries with the longest record of democratic government where the unions are strongest.

Perhaps the greatest contribution which should be made by Christians to the ideas which govern industrial relations is on the philosophy of work and the rewards for work. Is there any ideal to which we can aim for the content of work itself or is work a drudgery to which fallen man is condemned? Are we to work by the sweat of our brow without hope of enjoyment or should we try to make work itself enjoyable? Is it a legitimate aspiration to reduce the hours of work, or is work a duty and leisure, strictly utilitarian, a period of recuperation of mind and body to help us to work more efficiently? Should we have no limit to our desire for greater wealth, or will there be a point where everyone has enough? And should we allocate rewards between individuals strictly on effort, or on effort and inborn skill, or, as it is today, on effort, inborn skill and inherited wealth? Must we leave some element, even in an ideal world, for the chance supply and demand of the market and how much, if anything, should we leave over for those with no inherited wealth, no inborn skill and, by chance of upbringing or environment, incapable of sustained effort?

Mankind seems meant, in Christian teaching, to work as steward of God's creation and to put into this work all its skill and resource. The Christian also believes that one day in seven must be set aside for rest and for worship of God since man is a spiritual being and needs refreshment of mind as well as of body. The Christian believes too that man is made in the image of God the Creator and it would seem to follow that man has a creative instinct and, if it is allowed to develop, creative ability.

Those who do routine and repetitive work tend today to achieve a progressive reduction of hours of work while those with managerial skills find themselves working longer and longer hours. This must partly reflect the satisfaction which people find in creative work and the dissatisfaction of routine work. A manager does not stop working when he leaves the office; if he does not take his briefcase home, he takes his problems. The university teacher, the public servant, the artist and the writer all disregard the formal hours of work. But to the man working in a repetitive job on a machine, a job requiring little training, no imagination and no creative ability, life does not begin until the job ends. To him the hours of work are critical. We might aim, therefore, for a gradual change in working methods coupled with an advance in the educational system to reduce the number of people required for purely routine work and increase the number required for work requiring intelligence and initiative. This is probably the trend in industry anyway. Industry's demand for skilled men appears to be insatiable. The more complex machinery becomes, the more people are required to service and maintain it and the fewer people are required just to run it. The more companies invest in complex plant, the more the cost of their goods is made up of the cost of plant and the less is represented by the daily cost of operating it. So in the future men will spend more time in the creative work of building something new and less in the uncreative work of tending a piece of routine machinery. But if we do not do something to train people in creative skills, we are going to be left with a great divide in society between the skilled and the unskilled. Since the completely unskilled are already a minority in some countries, we will have to take exceptional care to see that the untrainable minority are not oppressed and that the trainable majority are in fact trained.

In addition to making the work in official working hours more creative there may, at the same time as official working hours are reduced, be a tendency to use the increasing amount of freedom from organised work for doing work which men feel to be more creative, more in tune with their natural talents, even though it may not be so immediately rewarding. Forty years ago it would not have been possible for most working men to learn another language. They simply would not have had the time. But if official working hours drop to two-thirds or half of what they were forty years ago, then clearly a man has the opportunity, if he wants, to develop his personality and enlarge his ability and talent in a way which can benefit mankind in the long run even if he cannot sell his new found ability in the short run. This trend in self-development should be fostered so that it may be possible to do away almost completely with the most menial tasks, the equivalent of the biblical 'hewers of wood and drawers of water'.

What would the ideal society make of rewards? Christian doctrine states that 'the labourer is worthy of his hire'. It condemns in the most outright terms those employers who have failed to pay a proper wage for work done. We would hardly expect that eternal truth, meant for all men at all times, would go into much detail on differential rewards for skill and responsibility. But it is interesting that in instructing Timothy on the proper order in the Church, Paul tells him 'Let the elders that rule well be counted worthy of double honour, especially they who labour in the word and doctrine. For the scripture saith,

Thou shalt not muzzle the ox that treadeth out the corn' (I Tim. 5:17–18). I think that in the context 'double honour' means money as well as respect. This passage has no precise equivalent elsewhere and we should not therefore build too heavily upon it. But I think that it says enough to show that additional responsibility should be rewarded if it is competently handled. There is also perhaps the inference that if the responsibility is not competently handled, that is to say that if the ruler does not rule well, there is not the same entitlement to additional reward.

What is the place of inherited wealth in reward? The Christian faith recognises the rights of property. Two out of the ten commandments are for the protection of property. They are 'Thou shalt not covet' and 'Thou shalt not steal'. What a man earns he is entitled to keep.

Although the laws of ancient Israel do not, and indeed cannot, apply directly to succeeding ages they are very useful in showing how the basic commandments are worked out in a particular society. The Mosaic law enshrined the right of inheritance but qualified it heavily by laws against accumulation of wealth. Leviticus 25: 10, 17, 23–28 sets out this doctrine. 'And ye shall hallow the fiftieth year, and proclaim liberty throughout all the land unto all the inhabitants thereof: it shall be a jubile unto you; and ye shall return every man unto his possession, and ye shall return every man unto his family. Ye shall not therefore oppress one another; the land shall not be sold for ever: for the land is mine; for ye are strangers and sojourners with me. And in all the land of your possession ye shall grant a redemption for the land. If thy brother be waxen poor, and hath sold away some of his possession, and if any of his kin come to redeem it, then shall he redeem that which his brother sold. And if the man have none to redeem it, and himself be able to redeem it; then let him count the years of the sale thereof, and restore the overplus unto the man to whom he sold it; that he may return unto his possession. But if he be not able to restore it to him, then that which is sold shall remain in the hand of him that hath bought it until the year of jubile; and in the jubile it shall go out, and he shall return unto his possession.'

Although men were entitled to buy and sell in the normal way, the cumulation of fortune and misfortune, the chance of skill in a family would, over a period, lead to an accumulation of wealth in some hands and an equivalent reduction of the opportunities (which in an agrarian society were heavily bound up in the ownership of land) on the part of others. The law was that in every two generations the wealth in society should again be evened up so that everyone could once more start with the same chance. It would of course be quite impossible to reproduce this in today's complex society, but our latter-day equivalent is the tax on wealth or the tax on fortunes when they pass on death. Unlike the theory of Communism, the Christian faith gives to men the security of their possessions and the rewards of their effort for their own lifetime, and unlike feudal societies it lays down that there shall not be great accumulations of wealth in a few hands because, as Leviticus has it, 'the land is mine' or as Genesis has it 'The earth is the Lord's and the fullness thereof.' In most of the Protestant nations these ideals about rewards do guide society but in some places they could perhaps be followed out more fully. There is still a strong temptation to use our temporary bargaining power to get more than our fair share and there is probably still too much concentration of wealth in too few hands. But wealth is much more widely spread in the Protestant countries than in all the other non-Communist countries and the avidity with which the Communists are said to read Galsworthy's *Forsyte Saga*, a story of a family of property, may show how much a society feels the lack of security which is inevitable when the personal ownership of property is so heavily discouraged.

It is inevitable in a market economy that there should be some elasticity in personal rewards to reflect the laws of supply and demand. If expanding industries could not pay more to attract men from declining industries the whole business of labour redeployment would become very much more difficult. It is much easier to run down a labour force by the natural wastage which arises from men deciding on their own to leave one job and take another than it is by set-piece, formal, negotiated dismissals. Higher wages will persuade people to leave the land and go into industry, to leave one part of the country to go to another. Despite wage differentials many people will still prefer to remain in uneconomic employment but at least money is a lubricant which does help to achieve better economic performance. It is difficult (even for organised labour) to negotiate against the market forces and very much easier to negotiate with the market forces.

Societies where Christian ideas are strong recognise that market forces may allocate rewards on a socially unjust basis and therefore use the taxation system to even out personal incomes. If because of the whim of the market someone suddenly receives a colossal income, then they are taxed at a very high rate. At the other end, those who through no fault of their own are thrown out of work are given financial underpinning. Those who find themselves in the upper income brackets, especially those who have arrived there because of their own skill and hard work, often find this hard to bear. And yet in countries with a Christian background it is nearly universal. Indeed, it is in the feudal countries where rewards are least deserved on the grounds of skill and hard work that they are highest relative to the rest of the community. But the president of a large corporation knows quite well that his own effort and skill can improve the company's economic performance by at least ten times his own gross salary and sometimes even by a hundred or five hundred times his gross salary. In his view the top fifty thousand men in the country can make or break the country's economy and he often finds it absurd—and says so forcibly and at length to anyone who will listen—that the country should quibble so much about the rewards of its wealth-producing elite.

I remember once staying with a works engineer on the edge of Ilkley Moor in Yorkshire. He was a good Christian and not in the least covetous. He got up at the crack of dawn every day and worked hard to keep in order the antique plant of a large Yorkshire woollen mill. For this he earned something like £1,000 a year. I propounded to him the theory of the wealth-creating elite and the way in which they could add so greatly to the wealth of mankind. His reply was that he didn't object to his boss getting more, but he worked with him and knew him and he certainly did not deserve forty or fifty times more. The trouble with the genuine wealth-creating elite is that they are weighed down by others, with the same titles and formal duties, who take home far more money for a fraction of the contribution. The answer of the creative elite is that these other characters should be pushed out of business by tough competition so that only the fittest survive. The trouble about this theory is that it demands a much purer and more efficient market economy than anyone has so far been able to devise. It also fails to recognise that declining industries and companies in difficulties often need managerial talent much more than those which are riding the crest of the wave, and that in these cases it can take years for the results of commercial and managerial skill to become apparent.

Management skill exists, can be judged and can and should be rewarded. But at the moment large corporations are self-perpetuating oligarchies which fix their own reward and at present there is not much check on the level of rewards they fix. Increasingly there is the check of disclosure but I think that we should go beyond this and have some professional scale of rewards for industrial management, some objective standard so that outsiders can no longer accuse industrial management of taking all the gravy.

But the professional scales of our ideal society should include, for industrial management, a substantial premium for risk until there is a profession of management which can truly assess a man's performance. Until that day a man's career runs the risk of damage from the outside forces of the market over which he has little or no control. But there will still be the need for deliberate risk-taking, which marks the real difference between the industrial manager on the one hand and the doctor, professor, civil servant or soldier on the other. The latter do not and indeed should not innovate on the market as the manager does and therefore they do not run the same risks of market failure. Then there is the risk of obsolescent skill. A doctor will always be in demand but who wants a manager who has invested his fund of skill in a career in the railroad industry, once that declining industry has no further need for his services? Indeed, people are beginning to ask what they are to do with the scientists over the age of forty in industrial laboratories, when managements judge that their creative period is past when none of their experience qualifies them for the very different job of line management. Or again, pity the wretched manager not responsible for final board policy whose company is taken over by a larger enterprise and who finds at the age of forty-five or fifty that the work he has been doing for years is duplicated by someone in the other organisation. He is given a polite hand-shake, a bit of money and told to go and do the best he can. In a year's time he is looking for a job at a quarter of his old salary. But while his earnings were high, progressive taxation sliced off the larger part of his risk premium and he was left with next to nothing. The manager is meant to take risks but he is taking risks not only with his shareholders' money but also, in the world as it is, with his own career. The shareholders can spread their risks but he cannot spread his. (The uneconomic attempts of companies to diversify rather than to concentrate their skills reflect, to my mind, the anxiety of the managerial class to spread their risks.) If the risk comes off, progressive taxation takes away the premium, although this is his security against the risks which do not come off and if he takes a risk which does not come off he then has no financial premium on to which he can fall back. It is, I think, a mistake on the part of society to remove from those people, who must for the benefit of society take risk decisions, the personal financial premium for the risks which they take. If this premium is removed then the correct entrepreneurial action is to take no risk, and risks will only be taken out of a sense of duty or by those who are quite remarkably competent. Where either duty or super-competence are missing, the managerial hierarchy of the large corporation will be strongly allergic to taking risks and where they must be taken, the responsibility will be well spread round and decisions will be taken not by individuals but by bureaucratic committees.

In arguing for a risk premium for industrial management I am not arguing that they should spend the premium on riotous living; indeed this would cancel out its proper function as a reserve. But if our progressive taxation were not on personal income but on personal expenditure then the premium could be given without changing the principle of progression. And to me it is more sensible that a man should be taxed on his expenditure, which is the measure of what he takes out of the economy, rather than on his income which is the measure of what he puts into it. If personal expenditure above a certain income, say £7,000 or $20,000 a year, were taxed, this would admittedly be more complicated than taxation of income. It would need a statement of capital assets at the beginning and ending of the year; but a good deal of this information now has to be filed for Capital Gains Tax. Industrial management could keep a large part of their gross income untaxed until they spent it. This would give them the risk premium they need, help them to take the risk decisions business demands and all this seems to me to be worth the cost of additional clerical labour. If it were not worth the cost, then there is something to be said for much lower rates of progression on income.

What pattern of earnings would the ideal society demand for the industrial worker? Is the argument of the unions right that men and indeed women should be paid 'the rate for the job' regardless of their age or sex or should we try to write into our wage structures a pattern reflecting social needs? The company in Japan which has taken some of its tone from Japan's more feudally based society is much more paternalistic and feels a greater responsibility for its workers. Not only is security of employment higher but the company is more able to pay its wages in a pattern reflecting the needs of its workers. In Western industrial society the 'rate for the job' is accepted largely, I believe, because this happens to suit economics rather than because of union demands. The 'rate for the job' would require a higher payment to women, but women are not in a position to enforce this payment in the market and they do not get it. The 'rate for the job' demands equal pay for unskilled or semi-skilled work to a youth of eighteen and a father of thirty-five to forty with family responsibilities. The eighteen-year-old may do the job just as well as the man of fifty-five

whose physical strength may be failing and the market rates
them both equally. But should society really pay enormous
wages to the teenager who has no family responsibilities, who
still lodges with his parents and whose income is therefore
almost entirely free to him to dispose of as he wishes? It is this
high premium payment to those who do not need it which has
resulted in a great deal of the disruption to family life caused by
industrial society. Even if we wished to stick to 'the rate for the
job' it would, I think, be perfectly possible to put a portion of
his wage packet in compulsory savings to be paid out progressively after he is twenty-one.

But if we abandon 'the rate for the job' it should be possible
to have an earnings pattern for wage-earners with a progressive
scale dependent on age similar to the earnings pattern for
salary-earners. This would not only allocate income on the
basis of the greatest need but the annual increase for age might
also take some of the pressure off inflationary wage demands.
After all, if you get your highest salary as a teenager it does not
give you much to look forward to for the rest of your life and it is
small wonder that this pattern of earnings produces unrealistic
pressure for higher money incomes. The third benefit would be
the reduction of the differential between wages paid to teenagers for unskilled work and the much lower income paid to
those who are learning a skill. Despite the fact that the demand
in the future will be for skilled work the pattern of rewards to
teenagers greatly discourages them from learning skills and
encourages the 'drop-outs' from the educational system. We
ought not to stick too rigidly therefore to 'the rate for the job'
but would have some progression of income from youth to age
and some hold-back of teenage income to be repaid when they
were likely to have the expense of marriage and children.

This is not quite so revolutionary as it sounds. Most income
tax systems already incorporate this system, taking more from
the bachelor, less from the married man and less still from the
family man. So the net wage after tax already takes social
responsibilities into account. No single company could hope to
take social responsibilities fully into account in negotiating a
gross wage, but either the company or the State might offer

attractive savings schemes for teenagers, which would be repayable progressively through their twenties and thirties. In Britain at present most companies have to pay a training levy and those with higher than average training bills get proportionate refunds from the levy. This should enable firms to be more generous in the amounts which they pay to apprentices and trainees and should lower the differential between teenagers learning a skill and those doing unskilled work. However, any increase in gross wages to take into account age and responsibility in society would probably require agreement between management and unions in the framework of a comprehensive prices and incomes policy.

The ethics of an industrial society cannot be laid down in black and white for all time. All we can hope to do is to follow the biblical pattern of setting out general principles and then applying them in detail to some of the problems confronting us at a moment of time. But we cannot claim that these applications are inspired. All we can do is to ask those who disagree with us to set out their own case and state their own reasons. A public discussion of such issues could do nothing but good. There will be those who underestimate the power of influence and example, who will argue that their objectives are unrealistic and unattainable. There will be those who so suspect the business community and the labour unions that the strictest and most detailed legal control is hardly enough. Somewhere between the two are our attainable objectives.

(iv) THE LAW AND SOCIAL STANDARDS

The social framework of society affects the Christian Church and is affected by it in many areas of life. We have looked at the great issues of government, of war and peace and of human relations in industry. Because the Christian faith should affect every part of life, it is hard to know where to stop. Perhaps the best way is to look at a few more cases where Christian standards and ideals seem to matter to the community and the extent to which these standards can be embodied in the law of the land.

The countries of the English-speaking world all have a basically Christian culture. Even if some were founded, as America was founded, as secular states, the founding legislators nevertheless adhered to Christian concepts and the law of the land is still mainly based on those concepts. Christian-based law, for instance, favours monogamy and respects the rights and dignity of women. Under Mohammedan law polygamy is legitimate and women have an inferior position to men. How should we reconcile the beliefs of non-Christians with a law based on Christian principles? I believe that if a country's original law was based on Christian principles it is right to seek to maintain those principles. Thus, if society is based on monogamy, it is right that monogamy should continue to be enforced except for those who enter the country already bound under polygamous marriage contracts. There was a case recently in Britain where the Hindu husband of a German woman died. Under Hindu law the property falls to the brothers and not the wife so the brothers entered the wife's house and took it over. Under British law the wife's interests are safeguarded and it seems right that while living in Britain she should be entitled, as she was, to the protection of British law.

These are cases where a minority belief is not a private matter but has become a public matter involving the laws of the land. To have different laws depending on a man's religion would run the danger of people changing their religion to suit their legal convenience, or indeed of inventing new religions in order to have the law altered in ways which suited them. Until the Reformation and for a hundred years afterwards men found it impossible to see how Protestants and Catholics could be accommodated under the same civil rule. Gradually men learnt how different forms of Church government could live within a civil framework still based on an underlying Christian culture, which no one disputed. It still has to be proved that we can go beyond this and base our underlying law on completely different philosophies. Private choice can extend to all those areas of a man's life which affect his worship and private conduct but not, if society is to retain any cohesion, to the law on which civil order is based.

This brings us to the whole question of social legislation. If we accept, as indeed we should, that we cannot make all sin punishable by law then some things which are sinful must remain legal. Two rules guide us in making this division. One is the rule that crime must be proven. You can prove that a man has stolen his neighbour's goods, but you cannot prove that he has coveted them. The one sin requires outward actions and the other does not. The one sin can be seen by our fellow-men and the other, although suspected, remains in the mind of the sinner. Our Lord has told us that sins of the mind are just as much sins. He told us that whoever 'looketh on a woman to lust hath committed adultery with her in his heart'. But adultery can be proved and lust cannot. It is therefore possible to have laws about adultery, and we do. But it is almost impossible to have laws about lust. Nevertheless it is still possible to have laws about actions which most people agree would arouse lust. It is therefore possible to have laws banning pornography. The question then for argument is whether a particular publication is likely to arouse lust or not.

But here we come up against our second rule which says that all law requires a substantial measure of public support, because laws without public support cannot be enforced and so can bring the whole apparatus of law into disrepute. Prohibition in America brought the law into disrepute and delivered whole districts in important cities into the keeping of armed criminals. But before we therefore conclude that whatever a lot of people want to do must be made legal, we ought to look at the results of new legislation on gambling in Britain. It was argued that almost everyone in Britain gambled and that even churches ran sweepstakes and lotteries in order to raise funds. Bookmakers existed in large numbers and most plants had their 'bookie's runner'. There was a little bit of strong arm stuff, but not much. However, it was held that the gaming laws were absurd in their distinctions between legal and illegal gambling and that what was open to a church to do privately, with a lottery in the garden fête, should be open to commercial interests to do in public. And so the law was changed, bookmakers were licensed and the so-called 'absurd distinctions' between legal and illegal gambling were abolished. But far from bringing the law into better repute by enabling garden fête lotteries to spread peacefully across the country, Britain has become an international gambling centre, the international gambling syndicates have moved in and territory for protection and other rackets has been acquired not by the old-fashioned scuffle in the streets of Soho, but by organised gang-land executions from which Britain once thought it was immune. We must still observe the rule that the law needs public support, but this principle should not be applied mechanically to legalise everything for which there appears to be a demand. No one can legislate for the abolition of evil but we can legislate to make our country a community where evil is not encouraged.

Religious education comes in to the uneasy half world which is neither wholly public nor wholly private. In Britain it is still compulsory to have religious education in State schools and in America it is compulsory not to have religious education in State schools. No doubt both countries want their young to be taught a basic morality and regard this as a public interest. In America there is an active religious community able and willing to undertake this outside the State system. In Britain, where the Churches are too weak to undertake it, the Head of State remains the head of the State Church and the State is formally Christian. This combination of circumstances probably accounts for the compulsory religious education in State schools. Ideally children should be taught religion in their Churches, but if their Churches do not teach them, are they to be taught no morality at all or should some attempt be made by the State schools to teach them that there is a moral order? Is it better that the Christian teachers of religious instruction, who are too few to cover all the children, should be supplemented for religious education by those who do not believe the faith? Or rather than be taught by unbelievers is it better that children should be taught nothing? Christians are sharply divided; yet if the void of faith is not filled by Christian teaching, however inadequately given, it may be filled with something else. At the best, the teaching of Christianity can light a spark in a child's life which will never be put out and at the worst the teaching of

Christian morality, even if inadequately done, will teach a child that there are absolute standards in life beyond his own passing fancy.

What should be done about the enormous urban sprawl which industrial society has made possible but has not been able to organise or to master? The ideal community should be socially mixed. People living together should know each other. I believe therefore that we should use the enormous advances in communications to move the job to the worker rather than the worker to the job. This goes against the apparent economies which come from mobility of labour. But if these economies are purchased at the expense of a lopsided and neurotic society then they are purchased at far too high a price. Just because the market does not put value on a balanced community it does not mean to say that a balanced community has no value. No one in his senses would carry a defence of the market economy to the point of saying that a commodity without a price-tag has no value. The commodity may just not be available or because of the conditions under which the market operates it may only be available to millionaires. The balanced community is not available on the market because the market, unaided, is not able to supply it. But if society as a whole wants a balanced community and is prepared to use zoning and other laws to achieve it, then of course it can have it. A democratic community can in the end have whatever it wants to have within its total resources, and a balanced community is within the total resources of most democracies today.

The great conurbations are less necessary today than they were. In the old days the merchant had to be physically present in the market place and to stand or sit down together with his fellow merchants. Today it is all done by telephone and indeed, in the money markets of the world, transactions are carried out every day over thousands of miles. In the old days the great assembly plants had to have satellite industries, their suppliers and sub-contractors all within twenty or thirty miles. The pattern of their work was so interwoven and they were so dependent on one another that the hazards of distance could not be allowed to intervene. However, today with the high-speed motorways and air-freight, distance is no longer the same hazard. In the old days managers had to have plants within a day's journey and that meant a hundred miles, but with the jet transport of today you can go six hundred miles and back with the greatest of ease. If the closely knit schedule of modern airlines does not quite fit, then for a big multi-plant company there is the private executive aircraft. The complexes of the Ruhr, of London, of Lancashire, of the eastern seaboard of the United States or of Los Angeles are becoming industrial anachronisms.

Yet if the creation of these conurbations has produced a mobility and anonymity which can destroy the cohesion of society, we would have to be careful in attempting to set up a more ideal balance not to swing to the opposite extreme of the company town where a small community is dominated by one great company to whom all its citizens are directly or indirectly beholden for employment. The new towns in Britain have succeeded in achieving a balance of employment and in none of them is one great company predominant. Many of them have major plants but all of them have a wide range of employment. Britain's new towns are by no means an ideal pattern because those who live in them have been uprooted from elsewhere, but in getting balanced employment the opportunity to change jobs and freedom from the dominance of one company, they have set off in the right direction. It ought, therefore, to be possible to have communities large enough to avoid the dominance of a few big companies but small enough to give some cohesion to society.

The ideal community should have a place for the old as well as for the young and it should not segregate richer and poorer in the vast one-class district of the modern city. That is not to say that people with different tastes and habits should be jammed together regardless of their views. That would be stupid. But rich and poor should be part of the same community, should be seen to be neighbours even if neither of them want to be near neighbours. This is not as idealistic as it sounds. Within a mile of Westminster Bridge and Big Ben, rich and poor are completely mixed up. The rich live in Vincent

Square and Smith Square, in small and expensive houses or
large and expensive apartment blocks and the poor live in
between the two in Page Street and Peabody Buildings. The
same is true of Chelsea and of the formerly poverty-stricken
area of Islington. This produces what is sometimes known as
the 'village' atmosphere of London. But the centre of London
has not been allowed to decay and it is not a typical city of
industrial society.

It is not only physical communications which have cut apart
the texture of society; the mass media of radio and television
have had a similar effect. In a sense both radio and television,
by bringing entertainment into the home, have kept the family
together. Whereas before it was necessary to go out for entertainment, now the family can enjoy it together. But the real
problem is not the place of entertainment but its form. It used
to be said that religion was the opium of the people. This is
clearly not true today, when the title must certainly go to
popular entertainment. There are strong arguments for some
control over the content of programmes over mass media.
They can be exercised either by sponsors of programmes alone
or by an independent authority either running or regulating
those who run the programmes. The non-commercial British
Broadcasting Corporation runs all its own programmes and in
Britain the commercial television programmes are regulated
by the Independent Television Authority which every six years
can take away a contractor's licence—and indeed in the 1967
review has taken away the licence of one major contractor and
cut two others down sharply. Programme sponsors in America
can take these duties seriously too. I remember several years ago
having dinner with an architect and his wife in a large studio
apartment overlooking Central Park, New York, and our
hostess had just come back from rehearsing a Greek tragedy,
which was going out for three hours on a New York station,
sponsored by a major company on the New York Stock
Exchange. But my impression is that it is exceptional to find a
sponsor who will put on a three-hour programme of Greek
tragedy, and that the soap opera is more usual.

It can be argued that although soap operas may be moronic

they are, under sponsor's discipline, a great deal more moral than some of the plays appearing on the British Broadcasting Corporation, and that people are more receptive to advertising and more likely to buy after watching a happy and moral ending than after a play which wrecks all illusion and innocence. Why, it can also be argued, should the State own radio and television stations and not control the theatre, the cinema, magazines, newspapers and books? Hollywood has its own code of morals and *The Sound of Music* came out of an uncensored film industry, whereas the boom in destructive satire was nurtured in the publicly-controlled British Broadcasting Corporation. And then there is the final argument against the regulation of public taste: that people will in the end get what they want and, to fail to give it to them, is only to ensure that they get it in some different way. British sound radio, it can be said, went on its prim maidenly way until public demand produced the pirate stations, and disc jockeys had to get good sea legs. Radio Caroline and Radio London wallowing in the North Sea just outside the three-mile limit were the stations to which British teenagers tuned in while the British Broadcasting Corporation radio turned out its more sedate programmes.

These are formidable arguments, and yet there are arguments the other way. First let us take the difference between broadcasting and other communication media. Broadcasting is enormously expensive and there are a limited number of wavebands, so that while not a monopoly it is always likely to be a near monopoly with a limited number of channels and stations available in any one part of the country. It is therefore quite unlike books and magazines where there is an enormous range of consumer choice to cover all tastes. But the essential difference is that sound radio and television go right into the home and are available to any member of the family, however young and innocent, at the flick of a switch. It is their immediate availability to anyone, however young, which calls for a measure of protection. If adults who consider themselves mature (though who is mature and what maturity is are matters for argument) want to go out and see, hear or read strong stuff, then they can do so; but there is no reason why it should be

laid on for them in such a way as to inflict damage on those
for whom it is quite unsuited. Society's interest in broadcasting
is far wider than economics. I believe, therefore, that any company wanting access to the wave-bands should, for the general
good, be given this power only under a licence which by its
terms protects the general public. What exactly these terms
should be is a matter for long and complex argument. The
licence should certainly include terms which will not only
protect the broadcasting companies from control by central
government and give them a real and genuine independence of
government, but it should also ensure that the means of
communication are not unduly influenced by the private
interests of those who control them. Both these safeguards are
present in the British system. Yet no Christian in Britain can be
happy that some parts of British broadcasting have not added
some impetus to the corruption of British life. Safeguards are
little use unless they are used and they will only be used if
enough people in society are both concerned and prepared to
act on their concern.

But what of the gutters of pornography, which seem at
present to be in full and odious spate? There are private and
public censorships, but are they effective and if not, is this a
matter of public concern or should it be left to private judgment? Communist, Catholic and indeed Mohammedan
countries have no hesitation in banning the lot. Mr. Khrushchev
professed himself disgusted by what he saw in Hollywood. A
look at a bookstall in Britain or in North America is not exactly
calculated to sell the Western way of life to a Communist with
genuine ideals (and it is quite wrong to suppose that Communists do not have ideals).

Lust feeds on itself and the less there is the less there is likely
to be. 'Evil communications corrupt good manners' and it is
silly to think that without the evil communications the manners
will be just as bad. The mass media of industrial society have
allowed evil influences to travel more swiftly, more persuasively
and more insistently than ever in the history of mankind until
now. Although pornography does not go into the home as
easily as radio or television, it is still too accessible and Christians

should act with all the power at their command to stop the free sale on public bookstalls of much which is sold there now. Those who are determined to seek out evil, whatever the consequences and whatever people think, will continue to do so and no one will stop them. But not everyone is as determined as this in the pursuit of evil. There is a very genuine protection to society in putting evil just a little bit out of reach so that there is some pause between thought and deed, some time for reflection. Some time ago London cleaned up its streets by imposing crippling penalties for solicitation. It was said that there would be dire consequences. It was said that this was just to sweep immorality under the carpet and that it could do no possible good but would put a premium on organised crime and protection. None of these dire consequences seem to have occurred. London is certainly a pleasanter place for the innocent visitor and there is far less casual contact with this kind of evil. And hypocrisy is just that little bit more difficult.

But society is not only affected by law, it is also affected and, I believe, much more than it realises, by example and by leadership. The man who holds fast to his opinions and ideals despite all the passing moods and fashions of his fellow men will, in the end, make far more of an impact than he realises. Those who ride the waves of fashion in the end affect nothing. But those whose position is well thought out and based, above all, on life as it is will usually make their point in the end. The Christian position is essentially realistic. It takes human nature as it is and not as it would like it to be. It is not starry-eyed and therefore it is unlikely to be knocked off course. On the other hand, it is not, because it believes in the power of God, pessimistic and therefore it is not discouraged. But the great strength of the Christian position is that Christians themselves are given by God the power to live it out in practice and in the end it is what we do rather than what we say that will make the deep and lasting impact.

CHAPTER 8

Christian Action

BEFORE PLUNGING INTO action to set the world to rights, before
becoming involved in highly controversial and debatable issues
with the best of motives, we need to consider very carefully who
among Christians is entitled to act and how far we can go to get
our way. President Truman said that those who didn't like the
heat shouldn't be in the kitchen. The Christian may set out his
own ideals for temperance in politics but he should remember
that politics is not a temperate occupation. As soon as we begin
putting forward political views people will not only try to
blacken the views, they will try to blacken us into the bargain.
Now this may be perfectly all right for the individual Christian,
but it is most certainly not all right for the Church. The
Church, as a Church, should keep out of politics and should
leave the rough and tumble of the battle to the individual
Christian. Not only should the Church keep out of politics as a
corporate entity, but individual ordained ministers, Paul's
teaching elders, the men whose main job is to preach God's
Word, should keep out of current political controversy, otherwise those who hear them will confuse the eternal and unchangeable truths of the Christian faith with uncertain and
changing arguments about temporal affairs.

The truth of God is unchangeable, but our methods of
applying the principles of the Christian faith in the changing
human scene may be a matter of judgment and Christians may
well be found on both sides of the argument. There are many
matters on which argument may be technical rather than moral,
or in which the technical and the moral are inextricably mixed
up. The alteration of the value of a currency involves the moral
issue of obligation to holders of the currency, but involves banking and economic factors which are so vital to the final decision
that no churchman could be competent to judge it morally.

It is also undesirable to divide the Church as a Church by political argument. The Church must be able to contain all political views compatible with the Christian faith. The process of argument is highly controversial and divisive, even if, in the end, the depth of underlying Christian principle may bring Christians to roughly the same conclusion. But above all, no section of the community should be forced to regard the Church as its political enemy. Our Lord took no part in the political controversies of the day, though the Pharisees and Sadducees tried hard to entangle him. The most he would say was 'Render unto Caesar the things that are Caesar's and to God the things that are God's.' He would lay down the principle but would not be drawn on the detail. The Apostles too, the Church's first spiritual leaders, avoided political issues. Paul's views on slavery can, I think, be inferred from the Epistle to Philemon where he returns the slave to his legal master but hints that Philemon might release him for Christian service. But he did not make a direct attack on the law of the Empire which entitled one man to hold another as part of his property. Slavery was as abhorrent then as it is now — and as the Church grew stronger it gradually died out in Christendom but none the less the Apostles made no political pronouncements on it. Paul goes no further in Romans 13 than teaching the general principles on which the State functioned and instructing Christians to submit to its authority.

The Old Testament prophets may seem to set a precedent for political pronouncements by spiritual means. But these men were directly called and immediately inspired by God to give a particular message to a king or his people. No man today can claim the authority of Elijah, Elisha, Isaiah or Jeremiah.

If the Church enters politics it is, after all, a highly potent force. King Henry II of England was neither the first nor the last secular monarch to wish himself rid of a 'turbulent priest'. For the trouble with his Archbishop, Thomas à Becket, was that he clothed his political views with the full might and panoply of the Church of God. This lent his views a weight which they would never have carried alone and forced his political opponents to fight, not with the former adviser of the

138   THE CHRISTIAN CITIZEN

King, Thomas à Becket, but with the senior Archbishop of the English Church. The politician who is denounced from the pulpit is put into the same position as the army commander whose troops are fired on from sacred ground. He is tempted not only to attack them but also to call in question the special position of the ground they stand on. In the end they risk losing far more than they are attempting to defend.

A small dining club of which I am a member once asked a bishop to dinner. Some members of the club questioned the right of the bishop to express political views. He said that if he found that housing conditions were appalling in his diocese he surely had the right to say so. They were his flock and he was interested in their welfare. He was not making an attack on any political party but simply on the conditions as he found them. The political members of the club said that they thought that this was naive. At any given moment a political party was in power and was responsible for the housing conditions at the time. Any attack on the housing conditions was an attack on the party responsible. This was certainly how the public and press would take it. No doubt the party in power would like to improve the housing conditions. It should not be supposed that they cared for their constituents any less than he cared for his flock. But if they wanted more houses they would be faced with hard political choices. There would have to be higher taxes or other programmes would have to be cut. Unless he was willing to say from the pulpit where the money should come from, he was hardly giving the balanced view which one might expect from a bishop and was using the authority of his position irresponsibly. It was also pointed out to him incidentally that it was doubtful whether most of the bench of bishops held his political views. If he really pressed the view that all bishops were entitled to sound off from the pulpit on political issues then he might well find himself in a minority as the full weight of Church opinion swung into political argument. I must say that the bishop bore our attacks well and my feeling at the end was that he had lost his vocation and ought to have been a politician.

This is not a theoretical argument, a matter of mere historic interest. The Church has been deeply involved in politics in

Britain in our time. The province of Ulster especially has been bedevilled in its politics by the identification of political parties with their Churches. I suppose that the Protestants would say that the Catholic Church had put the weight of its authority behind the Nationalist Party, which wanted the province to be severed from its historic connection with the United Kingdom and joined to the small republic of Eire. And so the Unionist Party was inevitably identified with the Protestant Church. But recently, when Protestant extremism was causing embarrassment to an Ulster government bent on reconciling the historic breaches, a leading British Catholic politician told me that he regarded this extremism as in some degree a divine retribution on the Unionist party in Ulster for having used the Protestant Church and its support in the past to maintain itself in power.

Once the Church involves itself in politics for any reason, however good it may seem at the time (and I have no doubt that the Protestants in Ireland felt quite genuinely when Home Rule was proposed for Ireland that 'Home Rule means Rome rule' and that they were fighting for freedom of religion), then it is extremely difficult subsequently to disentangle the one from the other. To the provincial government responsible for a community two-third Protestant but one-third Catholic, two-third Unionist but one-third Nationalist, it would seem wholly right to heal the differences, mend the breaches, obtain the largest measure of national consensus and to live in amity with their neighbours, whatever their remaining differences might be. Good diplomatic relations do not imply approval. We have to live with our neighbours whatever their political views or whatever their religion. But to Protestant Churchmen, alarmed by the Oecumenical Movement and the trek of ecclesiastical dignitaries to Rome, the approach of Unionist (and Protestant) Ministers to the National (and Catholic) Ministers in the neighbouring republic bore sinister overtones. And it was difficult for them to see that to warn their fellow-ecclesiastics that theological differences with Rome were irreconcilable was something quite different from telling Ministers that political differences were also irreconcilable. But a generation whose fathers were brought up to regard theological and political differences as one and the same thing finds it hard to change and it may require a further generation of wise leadership of State and Church before the two are back in their proper stations.

If the leaders of the Church and those who preach from its pulpits ought not to take part in secular affairs, then the burden of Christian leadership in secular affairs falls overwhelmingly on the ordinary membership of the Church. This is an activity which not only cannot, but must not be left to the minister. It is, in fact, one of the major functions of lay Church members who are qualified in any way to take a lead in society. If they do not act, Christian views on the issues of the day will not be heard. They have a tremendous responsibility.

How is influence exercised in modern society and to what extent can the Christian use modern methods of influence? It is, of course, difficult to generalise from one country to another. But at least in democracies there are certain common factors. Influence seems to come to those who are prepared to work, to apply their minds and to be patient. In most communities there is a vast sea of indifference and actual decisions are taken by a minority of activists. But activists can be divided fairly sharply into two groups. There are those who are extremists. Their activism is entirely political. That is to say, it is based by definition on attitudes rather than on reason. They have influence because they put forward aims which a great many people think desirable without in any way attempting to answer the enormous problems which have to be faced in practice if those aims are to be achieved. Their influence tends to be limited to those who do not have to make decisions and they are little help to those who do make decisions. They will the ends but not the means.

The man in power, however, has no problem about desirable ends. His overwhelming problem is the means to those ends. Time and again in an argument I have heard the man who has to make the decision say 'Okay, okay, we all want that to happen, but *how* do we make it happen?' The extremist can, of course, get a substantial though ephemeral political backing and to the extent to which he can deploy this against those in power he may get some marginal concession to his point of view at the expense of other points of view. But to the embattled politician, struggling with the hard facts of life, the pressure group shouting its head off in pursuit of desirable ends, but not prepared to commit itself to the tough discipline of working out realistic means to those ends, is nothing but a pain in the neck. In public life as I have seen it, the man of influence is the man who can produce a workable proposition which is likely to be agreed upon by those who carry the weight of responsibility and which is defensible by the political leadership of the party in power. This is the source of influence of the permanent official and of what we know in Britain as the 'establishment figure' who is to be found on all the expert committees and commissions of enquiry.

It is no job of mine to defend the establishment figure. Many fair criticisms can be levelled against this type of person. They can be too neutral, too lacking in 'commitment', too willing to put the issue in terms of their own (unadmitted) preconceptions and too unwilling to change those basic preconceptions. But the experts can also be unfairly criticised because they insist on facing and in making other people face the unpalatable facts of life and those who will not face the facts of life are sometimes tempted to erect the fantasy of a mysterious 'establishment' which will not let them get their way. A minister who blames his failure on the 'establishment' is usually a weak minister.

However, it is not one's purpose to defend or to attack the expert, simply to say that his power is very real and that it derives from advice which is based on knowledge, thought and hard work. It is also based on the humility of not always believing himself right and therefore being prepared to listen to other points of view and to take them into account in the advice that he gives. Anyone who wants to exercise influence has got to be prepared to work for it. It seems to me that very few people are, in fact, prepared to work for it, and that a quite surprising number of people think that all that is necessary to influence is the airing of half-baked views in high quarters. This means that those who are prepared to work will be surprised at the speed

with which they get a real hearing. Day after day there land
on the desks of those in power—either in industry or government—memoranda, newspaper articles, letters, so-called re-
ports and studies, all of which purport to give the answers to
their problems, but which gloss over or ignore the real difficulties, the critical problems with which they are faced. The rare
report of intellectual integrity which faces these problems for
what they are and propounds solutions to them which are
practicable, realistic, workable and acceptable, which gives a
real insight into the pattern of events, a real understanding of
what is happening and why, is like an oasis in the desert.

The trouble, of course, is that little of this is appreciated
because those in power and especially politicians very seldom
say it. They are very polite about the letters we send them. The
successful chairman of a very large company, with ideas of his
own as to what was wrong, told me that he went to see a very
senior member of the government. The Minister, he said, was
full of charm, sympathy and understanding. He said that so far
as he was concerned he agreed precisely with the views put
forward. It was his dearest wish to do just what was suggested.
There were unfortunately certain temporary but inescapable
difficulties, but as soon as these had been removed my friend
must believe that the will and the resolution were there to do
just as he had suggested. They spent over an hour together and
afterwards he wrote him a most courteous and understanding
letter. This enormously impressed my friend until a week or so
later he spoke to another company chairman who had been to
see the same Minister about something different. Out of
interest they swopped letters and found that they had both
been sent absolutely identical and apparently standard letters.
Both chairmen were sadly disillusioned. Mind you, I have
worked with politicians who were prepared to use all their
powers of persuasion to show their visitors that they were
wrong, but normally the only genuine sign that you have
changed the course of events is not words but action.

In a democracy it is not only necessary to convince those in
power that you are right, you must also convince a substantial
section of public opinion. The man in power not only wants to

do the right thing, he wants those who put him there to believe that he has done the right thing. So he wants what he does to have general support. A government can take a few unpopular measures, but it goes against the grain. All else being equal, the more support the measures have the more likely they are to be taken. This is a tough assignment but there is no way round it that I can see. If you believe in democracy then you must believe in public debate on great issues. But it is one thing to go in to lobby the polite politician and it is quite another to convince a great body of your fellow countrymen. The one debate is carried on in a polite and sophisticated manner, but the other debate can be very rough. People can be badly hurt and a determined opponent will cast doubt on a man's reputation. This kind of debate is not only rough, it is tedious. Maybe you can get a slot on television and talk to millions of people for ten minutes. But real persuasion usually takes much more time, and to be effective, must be far more intimate.

Many Christians come to the job of persuasion in too pessimistic a mood. They see the world as set in its ways, they see the pervasiveness of evil, the fear, the hostility and scorn aroused by the law of God and the Christian message. It is not easy, but it is not impossible either. The first rule, of course, is that you must be right yourself. Our advocacy must be based on Christian truth, must take into account the facts of life today. The best way of doing this, I believe, is to set up a relatively small group — perhaps a dozen — who have the same end object in view but who will bring to it a wide variety of background and expertise. Such a group needs a chairman who will be tough, open-minded, logical and polite. In that group you need to develop all the arguments you are going to encounter later on and you must deal fully and openly with the best possible exposition of the case against you. Indeed, it is not a bad idea once you have got your own basic position settled — though perhaps not before — to ask along some articulate and persuasive exponent of the opposite point of view. If at the end you feel he cannot answer your case or that his own case is weak, then this gives you a real sense of security in putting your own case in public later. If, however, he makes your case look weak, then it is just as well to know at that point and before you have made a fool of yourself in public. Of course, in welcoming an opponent, especially a non-Christian opponent, into the bosom of your group you need to make sure that the argument does not degenerate into one about basic assumptions. What you want to do is to find out where his assumptions lead him and why your assumptions lead you somewhere different. Both of you therefore need to respect the other's basic position. Otherwise you would get nothing but confusion. In many ways the humanist looks much the same as the Christian. Many of our objectives are common. We are both anxious to relieve suffering and improve the lot of mankind. But the basic assumption of the humanist that there is no life beyond the grave and no authority beyond the human mind often lead him to very different conclusions, and unless both sides freely acknowledge their difference on these points, discussion will get nowhere. Indeed, one of the great troubles about the Christian Church is that it has sacrificed clarity of mind on differences to the woolly-minded notion that reconciliation is best achieved by ignoring fundamental differences, and this has put it in the public posture where it seems either to believe everything or nothing at all.

Study groups are, of course, best composed of those who have a common experience of the problem they are tackling. They can be groups of Christian politicians, industrialists, doctors, university teachers, or parents. Or they can be groups of people who have a particular interest, an interest in foreign affairs or in juvenile delinquency.

When the group has come to its conclusions it will probably want to publish these in some form or other, and the publication of a thoughtful book on a particular subject has no substitute as an exercise in long-range influence.

Taking the argument to a wider field does not normally involve a major public attack on the main opponents of your idea. If you cannot first persuade your friends you will almost certainly never persuade your opponents. Any action campaign must begin among those who should be expected to support the campaign. First of all, therefore, it is necessary to carry the

Christian Church with us so far as we can, so that when we go to a wider public we are speaking not just for ourselves, but for the body of the Church. Of course, in an age when the Church is partly aligned with secularism and is not prepared to stand on its own truths, we cannot be expected to carry all of the Church. But we should at least expect to carry that part which is still prepared to take a distinctively Christian position. The budding reformer may find himself bogged down at base, trying to persuade the members of his own home church, when his vision is already soaring to far greater things. But before he writes them off for their dullness and inability to see his logic and wisdom he should remember that they are not all that different in intelligence and ability from other voters and that if he cannot convince those to whom he can appeal, on Christian principles, he is unlikely to convince those with whom Christian arguments do not count.

Having carried our own constituencies so far as we can, we ought next to take the argument out to moderate opinion, to people who do not take a specifically Christian line but who are nevertheless prepared to listen and to be persuaded. This is the critical point in the battle to get things done. These, rather than our opponents, are the people who have to be persuaded. In most communities and certainly in democracies, it is this middle of the road opinion, people prepared to listen to both sides of the argument and prepared to swing one way or the other, who have the decisive voice. But they are swayed not by wild arguments, not by extremists' statements, but mainly by the weight of the argument and its apparent relevance to the problem they see round about them. Middle opinion supported the Reformation in Germany but did not support the extremists. Middle opinion supported Cromwell in England but would not support the 'Levellers'. They were prepared to tolerate the restoration of the monarchy under Charles II but not the extremities of James II, his brother. It may be possible for an extremist to capture a great political party but it is infinitely more difficult for him to carry the country. The moderate does not like to be bullied or stampeded, he likes to hear the case and to make up his mind.

10

In secular affairs I have no doubt that the appeal to moderate opinion is right. The most convincing argument is the one which goes nearest to the other point of view and still succeeds in demolishing it. The more extreme your argument, the more vulnerable it becomes. The extreme argument may sound fine on a party platform or within a coterie, but it does not really succeed in swinging anyone from one position to another. Yet in many ways it goes against the grain with Christians to appeal to moderate opinion. If we believe, as we do, that we are engaged in a struggle between the forces of good and evil then 'he that is not for us is against us'. You do not snatch people as 'brands from the burning' by moderate argument. We are accustomed to the dramatic contrast between the saved and the lost and we feel that we must reason, as Paul did before Felix, of 'righteousness, temperance and judgment to come'. But it is a great mistake to use the same tone of voice about every subject. The elder in the Church preaching from the pulpit should expound with all the authority he can command the full law of God. But it is precisely because when we enter secular affairs we are not proclaiming the full law of God with all the authority of the Church, but only the individual lay Christian's view of what is right in the circumstances, that we have to modify our tone of voice. For the minister himself to make pronouncements from the pulpit about the hours during which drink can be sold, in the same tone of voice as he uses to call men to repentance, does damage both to the Christian case in secular affairs and to the preaching of the gospel itself. On subjects where we may be wrong, where we have no right to call in aid the whole weight of authority of the Church, we do best to express ourselves in moderate terms to moderate opinion.

Despite the impact of modern communication media, I believe that the most effective way still of changing opinion is the straightforward talk with questions afterwards. You cannot answer back to the man in the newspaper; and a radio or television discussion is bound to be formalised, stilted and clipped. But a half-hour talk and a half to three-quarter hour question and answer session get the maximum audience participation and enable most of the difficulties in people's minds to be put and discussed with the speaker. This is far more exhausting in time and energy than either writing or broadcasting, but I believe that if you did a study of the men and women who had really changed the views of their generation, you would find that they had been quite indefatigable in speaking at a great number of relatively small meetings, going willingly wherever they were asked. There is, of course, a limit to which you can combine this with a career and it is therefore necessary that this kind of job be undertaken by a wide range of people capable of thought, argument and leadership and not be left to just a few.

To sum up, the issues of our generation as I see it are the preservation of the family as the cornerstone of society, religious toleration, the rootless society of the great urban sprawl and its transformation into a more socially mixed, more personalised society, where men know their neighbours and do not disappear into anonymity; the stability of the new nations; the creation of wealth to enable the Afro-Asian nations, the have-nots of the world, to make the economic break-through into self-sustaining growth; the upholding of the dignity of the individual in the massive new institutions of industrial society.

But none of our study groups and none of our writing, preaching, lecturing or broadcasting will be any good if we do not help the individuals immediately around us. Charity begins at home and the Christian must be seen to care for those who are his neighbours. Our great thoughts for the reformation of society must not allow us to pass by immediate need on the other side of the road. We must give our full support to our colleagues on the job; we must remember that our wives have no other husband, our children no other father, and they deserve our energy, time and love. We must give hospitality to the Church and care within the Church to those who are 'out of the way'. What we say will carry weight but it is the love and care of the Christian for those immediately about him which carries the final conviction.

Only the minority can go out and argue the Christian case in the forum of public debate. But this minority are, in human terms, utterly dependent on the impression created on the public mind by the behaviour and standards of the majority of the Christian Church. If the one supports the other, then the groundswell will be irresistible. It is one thing to argue in theory, it is another to live out the argument in practice. It is one thing to agree that we should love our fellow-Christians of all races, it is another thing to ask them into our home. It is one thing to argue for the family as a basic unit in society, it is quite a different matter to be patient with our children.

Let's just pause here and go into the detail. Charity begins at home. Do we adapt our way of life to family needs, take our holidays with them, go to the places they would like to go, to broaden their minds by adult company? Do we do all this but try to buy love at the expense of discipline? Family life is a discipline for the parents, but it is also a discipline for the children. The father is the head of the house and not the general dogs-body. Love and discipline go together. The parents who can command love and affection can also command obedience. It is the selfish parent who brings up spoiled and selfish children. But who can say all this better than Paul? 'Children obey your parents' and 'Fathers, provoke not your children to wrath'.

It is one thing to argue for Christian involvement in the community, it is another to practise it. If a stranger came to the community, would they find Christians in the Women's Institute, Christians in the Young Wives' League, Christians on the Parish Council, Christians among the visitors at the Eventide Home, Christians helping with the Scouts and the Guides and with raising funds for charity? Or would the stranger find that the Christians kept strictly to Church activities and that no one in the community really knew who they were, what they did or what they thought?

Whatever our arguments, whatever our actions, they must arise from Christian doctrine. The drive and power must come from the Holy Spirit. We must be humble and not opinionated. We must be prepared to find that we are sometimes quite wrong and be able to admit it. We serve our fellow-men because of our love for a Lord who gave His life for us, a debt which, however well we serve, we can never repay. So whatever we do, we do it from a sense of duty and because it is right. We do not, like the cults, claim instant satisfaction. We do not, like the salesman, guarantee success. The Christian's time-span is not mortal. One sows and another reaps. One labours and another enters into his labours. One day with God is like a thousand years and a thousand years like one day. The Christian knows the meaning of patience and of endurance. But he also knows the meaning of action.

Christian Authority

THESE ARE DAYS in which Christians are deeply divided on the nature of authority, days therefore when it is necessary as never before to state one's assumptions — rarely though this is done.

There are three main sources of authority for Christian doctrine. One is the divinely inspired revelation which we find in the books of the Bible; one is the tradition of the Church handed down through twenty centuries of Christianity; and one is the capacity to reason which God has given us and which we must use to apply biblical authority and Church authority to the needs of our own generation. I think that all branches of the Christian faith would agree that these were the main sources of authority and that all were valid sources. But today we disagree most deeply on which source, in any apparent conflict between sources, should have the ultimate authority. The Catholics and High Churches give the last word to Church tradition. The Protestant liberals and modernists give it to human reason and the orthodox Protestants, among whom I include myself, feel that for the last word we must always go back to what God Himself has said in the Bible. They believe that we can neither put Church tradition higher than God's original instructions, nor pit the mind of man against the mind of God. They believe too that the Bible is the Word of God and that it is difficult to take any other view and still call ourselves Christians. Our Lord Himself believed the Old Testament, for He taught from it and said that He had come to fulfil it. He commissioned the Apostles who gave us in the New Testament the teaching He had delivered. The specific authority of each one of them was that they had seen Christ, who had been crucified and whose body had been put in the tomb under an armed guard, rise again from the dead — as both He and the Old Testament prophets had foretold.

Those who cannot accept the authority of the Bible as God's Word have got into their difficulties either because they do not bother to interpret it properly or more often because it conflicts with their own philosophy. If you start off believing that one Spirit, the third Person in the Trinity, inspired the whole of Scripture then you will look for accord in Scripture and you will have a coherent basis of interpretation. If you believe that Scripture was written by scores of different writers centuries apart in time and ideals, with no common source of inspiration, then you have no basis for interpretation, you will get into inextricable confusion and, as likely as not, conclude that the confusion is in the Bible rather than in your own approach to it. It seems worthwhile therefore to run over some basic rules of interpretation. This will give the reader some ground-rule against which to judge all the views which claim biblical authority. These are not my rules. They are the rules which I find are followed by all the great commentators on the Bible. They are not placed in any order of importance for all are important.

The first rule of interpretation is to compare Scripture with Scripture, to see how the passage you are examining compares with other passages on the same subject. This is the way to build up the thread of connection which we know as doctrine. Each passage gives a different illustration to the doctrine. They all complement and qualify each other and taken together all the passages about a particular subject give a four-square base on which to stand a major doctrine. Always suspect a view which is based on an isolated and unsupported proof text. These are the stock in trade of cranks and heretics.

The second rule is never to add to Scripture what is not actually written. This is the error of much Church tradition, Protestant as well as Catholic. Church tradition is a useful guide in matters of doctrine—though a poor guide to ceremony which should be adapted to the needs of each generation. We should always suspect a doctrine which has been held to be heretical throughout the centuries, but which is suddenly discovered to be true in the last fifty or a hundred years. Calvin did not hesitate to test Catholic doctrines of the sixteenth century by Catholic doctrines of earlier centuries. We may well find, as he did, that some traditions which come dressed in the garments of great old age are new ideas which somebody thought up not so long ago. But as St. John said in Revelation 22: 18, 'If any man shall add unto these things, God shall add unto him the plagues that are written in this book.'

The third rule comes out of the very next verse, 'and if any man shall take away from the words of the book of this prophecy, God shall take away his part out of the book of Life, and out of the holy city, and from the things which are written in this book'. The third rule is, therefore, that we ought never to take away from Scripture what is plainly written there. This is the sin of the Protestant liberals and modernists but it is also in large measure the sin of some of the more extreme dispensationalists. If you find that at the end of a long and involved process of dispensational reasoning whole portions of the Bible such as the Ten Commandments and the Sermon on the Mount are said to be irrelevant to the world today then you have every reason to be mighty suspicious of that teaching. At this point the fundamentalist is committing the very error which he so strongly condemns in the modernist.

The fourth rule, which many would put first in importance, is to take the passage in its context. We have to decide the relationship in which the words were said and then see whether this can be applied to other relationships or solely to the passage in the context. Both Catholics and dispensationalists are apt to weave great theories on quite inadequate words. There are allegories and types in the Bible but a lot of people today make allegories and types where there is no evidence for anything else but a plain straightforward story. When Our Lord was on His way to the Mount of Olives on the night of His arrest His disciples said to Him (Luke 22:38) 'Lord, behold here are two swords. And he said unto them It is enough.' On these simple words there were those in the medieval Church who created a whole theory of the equal power of Church and State to bear arms, to coerce and to punish. They said that the two swords were symbolic, that one represented the power of the State and the other the power of the Church. I believe that the passage simply meant that Our Lord did not intend to resist arrest. This interpretation is borne out by His order to Peter to sheathe his sword when he struck off the High Priest's servant's ear. Protestants have made the same mistake. In the seventeenth-century religious wars in Scotland, some Scottish Protestants were apt to take God's commands to Israel for the extermination of their enemies as applying equally to the enemies of the Scottish Protestants. This attitude did not do the Protestant cause much good.

The fifth rule is to distinguish clearly between fact and symbol. People today are inclined to treat Adam and Eve as symbols for the origins of the human race but you also find people today who are prepared to treat Revelation as being quite literally true to the last jasmine stone. But Revelation is clearly labelled. It is stated to be a vision of the Apostle John. At points an angel appears to John to explain the vision and from this it must be accepted that what John sees is symbolic. Then there is the pattern of symbolism which says the same thing in different ways, for instance, three and a half years in one place; time, times and half a time in another, and in yet another place it is 1,260 days. The symbol of restless humanity is the sea and the precious metals and precious stones symbolise something which endures for ever. To take all this quite literally is to fly in the face of the evidence.

On the other hand, those who regard Adam as symbolic are in grave difficulty in the passages in which he is compared with Christ. 'As in Adam all die, even so in Christ shall all be made alive.' If Adam never existed, how can this comparison be made? If by the act of one man all were condemned, then by the act of one Man, Christ, all can be made alive. This is why Christ can die for all. But if Adam never existed and never committed the act then doubt is thrown on the key Christian doctrine that Christ's death was sufficient for all men. If it was not sufficient, then faith alone cannot save and our whole theology is undermined. I can see no reason in history or in science why there should not have been one man Adam, the head of our human race. It is not only stated in unambiguous terms that he lived and died, but a whole genealogical tree is linked to him and the actions of his sons are described in language far from symbolic. We may dislike the doctrine of original sin and this may make us prefer to treat Adam as symbolical. But the symbolism cannot be found in the text. The best rule is that we should be sparing with symbols except where they are clearly stated to be symbols.

The sixth and similar rule is that words normally mean what they say and say what they mean. It ought not to be necessary to have this rule but the Bible is a hard book for men to swallow and words sometimes have to be very plain indeed before men will allow themselves to be convinced that they actually mean what they say. The Bible says some very plain things about work. It also says some hard things about sluggards. But some people seem quite determined that these things are not what they seem and that there is, if only one can find it, a Christian doctrine of leisure. There may be one, but personally I have never come across it. I was once asked how the ordinary man could understand this book written thousands of years ago. I said that I thought the command 'Thou shalt not steal' was as simple and valid now as it was 4,000 years ago. Those who do not like it have to weave a lot of words before they can make it say something different.

The seventh rule is that where there are apparent conflicts whether scientific, moral, historic or textual, we should examine both the standing and authenticity of the conflicting material and the scope of the biblical statements. Sometimes it will be found that Christians have exaggerated the statement of the Bible and have made it say more than it actually does. When the poetry of the Bible speaks of the sun rising and setting it is not making a scientific statement and for the Church to base its scientific position on the poetry of the Bible is ridiculous. This is now acknowledged but there was a time centuries ago when it was not. More often today what is exaggerated is not the standing of the Bible's statement but the standing of the counter assertion. Some historical critics have treated the Bible as if it were the only unauthenticated record whereas it is probably a more soundly authenticated record than any other ancient historical source. It has been gone over with a fine-toothed comb by innumerable commentators and often what is produced as a difficulty which only the advanced thinking of the twentieth century has brought to light is dealt with plainly, simply and satisfactorily by any commentator from Calvin onwards.

Index